Prologue-The Boy Who Wa

Gravesend - Kent, 1956

The boy sat on the shingle long after the daylight had thinned, watching the tide pull itself across the beach as though the sea were tidying the world before nightfall. David Bentley, sixteen and growing into his height, dug his fingers into the cold stones and tried to imagine the shape of his future.

Out on the horizon a freighter moved steadily north, a dark silhouette against the last faint band of gold.

The Merchant Navy had been lodged in his mind for months now, a whisper that grew louder every time he stole another look at the horizon. He wanted to know what lay beyond Kent—beyond England—even beyond the maps he studied with almost religious attention. But to want something so obsessively felt dangerous, - almost indulgent.

The freighter's lights flickered and then vanished into the swell of oncoming night.

Years later, when David Bentley would stand on the deck of a ship half a world away or lie awake in a caravan on a Suffolk shoreline waiting for a morning he did not yet know would bring Julie Smith into his life, he would remember this moment. The shingle, the wind, the reluctant blessing from his father.

And the sea, calling him forward long before he knew where it would lead.

Chapter 1- First steps

During the long summer holidays in 1954 at the age of 14, David found a job in a part time job in a small engineering workshop in the Kentish village where he lived.

He adapted to the work immediately and showed interest in the machinery and activities.

The owner, Stanly Hawkins, became so impressed with David that he asked him if he would like to work for him full time when he left school. His was willing to offer David an apprenticeship.

David explained that his father would never agree to him leaving the grammar school as he wanted him to go to university.

David's father was born in 1898 in Irlam and never had the benefit of even basic schooling due to poor health as a child, so it was understandable that he wanted his son to make the most of his opportunities. He was planning for his son to attend the grammar school until he was eighteen.

But after David returned home that afternoon, he mulled on the offer Stanley had made about taking him on as an apprentice. He was thinking to himself.

"It's my 15th birthday two days before I am due to go back to school. I wonder if I would be allowed to leave if I could persuade my dad to sign the release papers from the school?"

And this thought grew legs over the following days.

Deep down inside, David would love to travel, to go to sea. He would often sit down on the promenade in Gravesend and watch the ships going up and down the river Thames. Containerisation in 1954 had not yet been introduced to the world of shipping. That would have to wait for a few years. Meanwhile, dry cargo was being transported by freighters which were labour intensive, and seafarers would throng the pubs and clubs in Gravesend.

This attracted David as he thought a seagoing career would be a far more attractive lifestyle than working in a factory or an office. But if this secret ambition was to become a reality, he knew there was a route to go, and this meant he had first to use the workshop opportunity as a stepping stone.

Across the river grom Gravesend was Tilbury docks and the Shipping Federation office outside the gates.

One morning, David took the ferry across the river from Gravesend and walked to the offices of the Shipping Federation.

There he spoke to a member of staff about the process he would need to follow if he were to find employment on a ship.

The officer explained to him the best way forward for a young fellow like himself and gave him an application form for entry into the Sea Training School in Gloucestershire.

Looking over the application document, he noted that he could not be accepted for consideration of training until he had reached 16 years of age. But as this was a little over 13 months away it seemed to him like half a lifetime.

But he kept the form and allowed the thoughts of a seagoing career to develop in his mind. Day after day the attraction grew, and he spoke to his mum about it.

She wanted him to continue with his education and tried to make him see how fortunate he was in the opportunity of a university education. No-one in the entire Bentley family had yet ever been to university, and it seemed a golden opportunity for him .

But David now had the obsessive thought of a seagoing career embedded in his mind. He was determined.

Eventually and after much pestering, he persuaded his mum to speak to his dad with the idea.

His father was very much against the idea saying that if he really wanted to make a career as a seafarer, then he would need to get accepted as a cadet by a reputable shipping company. He would be better equipped for acceptance at this level if he could show a few "A-levels" on his application form.

But David insisted that he could make his way through becoming a deckhand first. This meant a route through the Sea Training School at Sharpness Gloucestershire.

After much argument and exchange of idea over the next few days, his father, although disappointed, relented, and agreed not to stand in his way.

Chapter 2 – Sea Training

David left home in Kent early one Monday morning in September 1956 and caught the train to London. Everything he needed to take, - personal effects, clean underwear, and all were stuffed into a brand-new kit bag purchased from the Army & Navy store in Gravesend.

"A bit like going on holiday" he thought. But this was to be no holiday as he was to discover very soon.

After embarking the train at Charing Cross station, he took the number 44 bus to St. Pancras railway station where he boarded a train to Sharpness.

Arriving at around 18:00 I disembarked. There were about 20 other lads of his age who disembarked and who by their appearance were obviously there for the same reason as I was.

They were met at the station by an adult officer in Merchant Navy uniform and two lads who were dressed in the uniform that he was to wear every day for the next few months during my training. The group were instructed to form two columns of ten and were marched out of the station and up the steep hill leading to the training school half a mile away.

Approaching the school, David could see it was housed in an area surrounded by a high fence and there were Nissen huts dotted around the enclosed compound.

The most disturbing aspect was to see perhaps up to 100 boys being marched around in the parade ground with instructors bawling and shouting at them all the time. David was not expecting this kind of welcome and wondered if I had done the right thing by coming here.

In fact, two boys in out column would not enter the gates seeing this and they just turned around and literally ran down the hill back to the station. They had obviously seen enough. But no-one tried to stop them.

The boys were ushered through the gates and were taken to a reception Nissen Hut. The lads' personal details were processed, and they were lectured on what we had to do next.

Then they were taken to another Nissen hut where they were made to hand over the 5 pounds (£5), each of them had to bring, which would be doled out to them at 5 shillings (25p.) a week.

This was their pocket money, - (provided by their parents and NOT the Shipping Federation). After this they were issued with a bedsheet a blanket a pillow and pillowcase and marched off to another Nissen hut which was to be their billet for several weeks.

After this period was over, they would transfer to the training ship laying in the canal basin close to the River Severn. There were eighteen lads housed in this billet. Each boy was allocated a bunk bed. The toilet block was across the parade ground, and this is where the boys did their ablutions.

There were no showers in the block and every day the boys would be marched over there to wash. They would strip naked and partly fill a basin with water which they would splash over their bodies and use the soap provided to lather. If they took too long about it, one of the sadistic instructors would walk down the rows of naked lads and slap them across the bare buttocks with a slipper. They perhaps did this to emphasise the power they had over the boys or even a form of sexual gratification.

After this ritual it was time to rinse off, clothes back on and marched back to their billets. To some of the lads it was harsh, but they soon got used to it.

This was all part of a discipline which they all resisted at first but later, a lot later, David came to recognize as necessary and was in fact a good character builder.

He would not admit this at the time but as he got a few more years under his belt he felt gratitude for the tough experiences that were meted out to him in those days.

For example, all the huts were heated by coal burning stoves which had a steel pipe going through the roof for a chimney. The coal was delivered each week by trucks and tipped into a corner of one of the open areas in the camp.

One day, David was caught fighting with a boy from Glasgow who was always giving him trouble when he had his mates around.

As a punishment, the two lads were made to collect lumps of coal from the heap, wash each piece, and the whitewash each piece. Then, they had to stack each piece in a neat and orderly pile.

They were, (naturally), made fun of by other lads during this exercise, and it took three days of this activity before it was decided by the officer that they had been sufficiently punished. All this activity was carried out their own time after normal training hours, and they were mostly at this until they were ordered to the ablutions for washing the coal dirt from their bodies.
David learned how to slice hemp ropes, and steel wire rope as part of his training.
He also learned how to coxswain a lifeboat in emergencies, rig a bosun's chair, climb a mast, read a compass, and other such activities that he could expect to use when he was posted to his first ship.

Obeying orders was all part of the training along with strict time management. He was taught it was a cardinal sin to be late on watch and so these things became embedded in his psyche by the time he had left the sea school.

A few months after his arrival at Sharpness, David left the sea-school, anticipating his first sea voyage. He felt he was ready.

Chapter 3- The peanut returns

Arriving home he was greeted warmly by his parents and siblings. He wore his uniform with pride until his pals started calling him a "peanut" because of the wide bottom trousers and pea jacket which comprised the trainee uniform that he'd been wearing during his training period.

After a couple of days at home he gave in to peer pressure and resorted to abandoning his uniform. The drape jacket, the drainpipe trousers and chucka boots became the norm. He was again accepted as being *"back to normal"* by his pals.

After being home for some time, David received a telegram from the Shipping Federation.

He was to report to the Federation offices at Tilbury. It was a date to remember, - April 4th, 1957. He was about to embark on a career in the Merchant Navy.

On arrival he was given a medical examination by the doctor and issued with a Seamans Discharge Book complete with his photograph, which had been taken at the sea school.

He had several injections from the doctor to help protect him from things like yellow fever, typhus etc.

He was told to return home and expect instructions in the coming days.
Just two days later, another telegram arrived. He was to report to the Shipping Federation offices in Dock St. London complete with all his kit. He would then be allocated his first ship.

At Dock Street "pool", he was instructed to board a bus waiting outside. There were about fifteen other fellows on the bus and after a two-hour journey they arrived alongside a ship berthed at the Isle of Grain Refinery in Kent.

The ship was a tanker owned by the British Tanker Company managed by British Petroleum (BP).

He was directed with other crew members to the ships office where the Master of the vessel welcomed them onboard and offered them to sign on for the next voyage.

David signed on as "Deck Boy" and was told he was to receive a salary of eleven pound and seventeen shilling per month (£11.85). He was informed his conditions of employment was seven days a week at eight hours a day. Any hours over this would be paid at the rate of two shilling an hour (£0.10).

In the ships office, a copy of the "Ships Articles" were posted, containing the terms and condition that every crewmember was legally bound to.

These articles covered everything including quantities of food rations each crewmember was entitled to receive.

A summary follows:

1. Purpose of the Ship's Articles

The Ship's Articles—formally called the *Agreement and Account of Crew*—set out the **contractual terms** between the ship's master and each member of the crew.
By signing, a seafarer formally entered the service of the vessel for a **defined voyage or period of employment**.

The Articles recorded:

- The ship's name and official number.

- The intended voyage or service period.

- Each crew member's rank, duties, and wage.

- The rules governing conduct, discipline, provisions, and discharge.

2. Duties and Expectations of the Crew

Crew members agreed to:

- Perform all duties appropriate to their rank **efficiently and diligently.**

- Maintain conduct that was **orderly, honest, sober, and respectful.**

- Follow all **lawful commands** issued by the master and officers.

- Support the safe navigation, operation, and maintenance of the ship.

Seafarers were expected to always be ready for work required by the watch system and to carry out additional tasks in emergencies.

---

3. Discipline and Behaviour

The Articles incorporated standard disciplinary rules authorised under the Merchant Shipping Acts. These required that crew must **not**:

- Be intoxicated on duty or unfit for work.

- Engage in fighting, insubordination, or abusive behaviour.

- Damage or steal ship's stores, equipment, or cargo.

- Bring prohibited items or weapons aboard without permission.

Breaches of discipline could lead to **fines, wage deductions**, or formal entries in the **Official Logbook**, and serious offences could result in legal action.

---

4. Absence and Desertion

Seafarers were required to **remain with the ship** until properly discharged. Two forms of non-attendance were recognised:

Absence Without Leave (AWOL): Leaving the ship without permission.
Desertion: Leaving with the intention not to return.

Penalties (set by law) could include:

- Loss of wages up to the time of desertion.

- Monetary fines.

- Reporting to maritime authorities for further action.

---

5. Provisions, Welfare, and Living Conditions

The master was obliged to supply food and water according to the **Board of Trade's standard scale of provisions**.

Crew members had the right to:

- Sufficient rations and drinking water.

- Compensation if provisions fell short ("short allowance").

- Basic medical care for illness or injury incurred in service.

They were also responsible for maintaining cleanliness and following the ship's hygiene rules.

---

6. Wages and Allowances

The Articles set out:

- The **rate of pay** for each crew member.

- Conditions for **overtime, leave,** and **advances.**

- Lawful deductions, which could include fines, compensation for wilful damage, and certain medical or repatriation expenses if misconduct was involved.

Wages were typically settled at discharge before a **shipping master** or **British consul**, depending on the port.

---

7. Safety and Emergency Duties

By signing, every seafarer accepted responsibility to:

- Attend and participate in **lifeboat, fire, and emergency drills.**

- Assist in the protection and preservation of life at sea.

- Take all necessary action in emergencies, regardless of normal rank or duty.

The expectation of mutual assistance and readiness was a core part of merchant service.

---

8. Termination of Service

A seafarer's service ended when:

- The voyage or term stated in the Articles was completed, or,

- The master officially discharged them before the proper authority.

At discharge, crew members were entitled to:

- Wages earned.

- Any accrued leave-pay.

- A certificate of discharge, noting conduct and ability (as was common practice of the era).

On this vessel and every vessel David joined thereafter which was flying the "red duster", these were the general terms and conditions of employment.

Chapter 4 – First Voyage

David was shown by a cadet to his cabin in the after end of the vessel. The cadet told David to stay there for now and the bosun would call on him shortly.

David was impressed with his cabin which he has to himself -he did not have to share with another rating as he had fully expected. He began to unpack his gear and stow them away.

Later, there was a knock on the door came and there stood a short stocky fellow who greeted him. He introduced himself.

"My name is Mr. Scott. Now come along, I'll show you around and explain your duties."

"Yes sir" said David.

"Don't call me sir. That's for officers. Just call me bosun."

"Aye aye Bosun".

The first place the bosun showed David was the crew mess and pantry located on the port side of the vessel in the aft section. There he explained to David what was expected of him.

- To keep it clean and tidy.
- The deck to be washed every morning.
- The food for the crew to be collected from the galley and hot food placed in the bain-marie.
- Collect provisions daily from the ship stores.
- Ensure that fresh coffee was available throughout the day for the crew.

Then the bosun took him to the petty officers messroom and pantry on the starboard side of the vessel in the aft section. David was instructed to do the same things here as in the crew messroom.

Then he was taken to the deck crew toilet and shower block and told this had to be kept clean . The same applied to the petty officer's toilet and shower block.

Then on the crew recreation room. This was also his obligation to keep clean and tidy.

Then the companion ways and alleyways in the whole aft section. These had to be kept clean and tidy.

At the end of the tour, David asked the bosun who would be helping him do all this work.

The bosun just laughed. *"This is for you - and you alone. You will have time to get used to it and I'll not be too hard on you. But after one week, I shall expect you to have mastered it. After one week I shall not accept any excuses. I hope you understand this."*

This came as a shock to David. How on earth will I manage all of this in eight hours each day he said to himself. But he was determined to give the impossible a shot. He would try and try.

Right after the tour with the bosun, David got to it. He began to meet the crew as they drifted into the messroom. The ship had not yet sailed, and watch routine was suspended until it was time to go to sea.

He dished out mugs of coffee or tea when he was asked and at 4:30 in the afternoon began bringing in the food from the galley, located just outside the door of the accommodation are on the "Poop Deck"

The ships cook was a huge fellow from South Shields called Benson. Behind his back he was "Big Boots Benson", but that was never said to his face. Most of the crew called him "Doc" which was customary for cooks on merchant vessels to be called.

The title "Doc" derived from the sailing ship era when most cooks' onboard vessels were the nearest thing to a doctor. If and amputation was to be performed at sea, it was usually the ships cook who was called upon to perform the gruesome task. After all, a ships cook was used to carving up sides of beef or lamb etc whilst preparing the crew meals. So that's how the name "Doc" came about.

Another nickname that was traditional was for Deck Boys to be given the title "Peggy".

This derived from the sailing ship times when there might be a case of a sailor having an amputation and was subsequently fitted out with a "peg leg".

He was now unable to climb the rigging or many other tasks that required adequate agility and so was given the job of catering to the deck crews. This meant cleaning and serving the crew members.

And so, when crew members began calling David "Peggy" it had to be explained to him why. When this was understood he was able to accept the name without any problem any all.

When a couple of days after he'd signed on the ship had orders to sail, he was excited. He had a plateful of minced kidney for his meal before they sailed.

Later in the evening as they crossed over the North Sea on the way to Antwerp in Belgium, the sea was rough and for the very first time in his life, David became seasick. As a result, he vowed NEVER to eat minced kidney ever again.

Arriving in Antwerp, David had his very first experience of visiting a county other than England. It was exciting and he spent just a couple of hours in the city seeing the sights.

After about thirty-six hours the ship went around the coast to Rotterdam. He like this place. He found that almost everyone he encountered could speak the English language.

From Rotterdam the master received orders from head office to proceed to Abadan in Iran, which in those days was generally referred to as Persia.

During the voyage from the English Channel to Port Said, David gained a little experience in steering the vessel. He enjoyed this very much and even though he accepted at the time that his position on the ship was just a tad higher than a ships cat, he felt more a seaman than ever.

The Suez Canal was an experience different to anything he'd ever imagined. Before the ship could proceed through the canal into the Red Sea, it had to lay at anchor whilst documents were prepared, and a pilot arranged for transit through the waterway.

As soon as they anchored off Port Said, the ship was surrounded by small boats. These small boats were laden with merchandise produced locally.

There were small wooden camels, delicately carved and upholstered in brightly coloured leather.

There were the **"Gilly-Gilly-Men"**, magicians who could perform amazing "magic" shows for the crews for the price of just a packet of cigarettes. The smells and sounds were amazing, and David loved it all.

David wanted to take a turn at steering the ship through the canal, but the Egyptian pilot would not allow it as he did not yet possess a certificate of competency issued by the then **"Board of Trade."**

The Suez Canal was closed in November 1956 and started allowing traffic through in in April 1957. David discovered that his ship was one of the first to use it for transit from the Mediterranean to the Red Sea since the re-opening.

David's ship was part of a convoy that followed the leading vessel into the **"Bitter Lakes"** where they anchored for about 3 hours. This allowed a North bound convoy coming from the Red Sea to bypass them and travel on to Port Said and the Mediterranean Sea.

When the signal to proceed was given, all the vessels in the convoy shipped anchor and proceeded South towards Port Suez and the Red Sea.

It took them another six or seven days to reach Abadan in Persia - (Iran). There they loaded a cargo of crude oil and departed the port two days later. They were not allowed ashore, and this was a great disappointment for David. But most of the crew were not fussed about a shore trip as they had been here before and the knew it wasn't a very popular place with seafarers from western societies. They tried to assure David he wasn't missing anything special.

What David found fascinating as the ship traversed the Shatt-Al-Arab-waterway up to Iran was the tens of thousands – (perhaps millions) of palm trees. It seemed almost forest-like on both Iraqi sides of the waterway. It was phenomenal.

After loading a cargo in Abadan, the ship headed to Durban in South Africa.

For almost the whole trip the sea conditions were good and after about fifteen days sailing the shoreline of Africa became visible and soon after they were moored at the oil terminal on the "Bluff", a few miles from Durban city central.

David was allowed shore-leave with the rest of the crew, and he found Durban a lovely city to spend some time in. He went to the beach for swimming with his pals and had fright when he allowed himself to be taken by the strong current away from the protection of the shark net.

This shark net was placed in a specific area of the beach, and its position was indicated by two beacons on the shore about two hundred metres apart. There were notices on the beach telling swimmers to say within the areas defined by these beacons. Outside the area defined by these beacons was declared unsafe.

The lifeguards were posted on small towers that allowed them a clear view of the beach. If anyone veered too close to the edge of the safe area, the lifeguards would use the Tannoy system to warn the swimmer they were close to danger and to get back inside the "safe area".

This is what happened with Tony, and when he came ashore the lifeguards reprimanded him strongly, warning him that he was not only putting himself in danger but also the lifeguards too as they would have to deal with the situation if he had he got into difficulties.

These were the days of the assisted passage to Australia from UK for citizens who wished to emigrate to Australia and start a new life.

After WWII, Australia wanted to rapidly increase its population for economic development and national security. The Australian government adopted the slogan **"Populate or Perish"** and began heavily subsidising migration from the UK.

The aim was simple:

- Bring in young, healthy workers.
- Increase the English-speaking population.
- Strengthen cultural ties with Britain.

The scheme was called "Ten Pound Pom" because adults paid **£10** for the passage to Australia.

This made it one of the cheapest long-distance migration opportunities in modern history.

Many of the ships transporting these new adventurers to and from Australia from Southampton or Tilbury would call in at Durban on the way for fuel or necessary replenishments.

Whilst Davids ship was in Durban on one occasion, there was a Union Castle vessel in transit from Australia. It was now carrying freight to UK before returning to Australia with more immigrants. This is when David came across **trans-gender** people for the first time in his life.

He was in the aptly named Queens hotel one afternoon having a few beers with other crew members.

Suddenly, about fifteen fellows came into the bar. At first David thought they were women. They wore dresses and high heels and makeup on their faces and indeed looked very female. But it was revealed in short time that these were crew member off a ship called the **Adelaide Castle.** They were transgender crew members who had come ashore to party at the hotel.

David was fascinated by these people. They were hilarious, friendly, generous with buying everyone in the bar drinks.

David and his pals had a rally fun afternoon before it was time to return to their own ship which was due to sail that evening. It was an experience that David never forgot and opened his mind a great deal. Any prejudices against those who had a different lifestyle such as these transgender people were dismissed in one afternoon. He had always considered he had an open mind but now his perspective of humanity had developed even further.

Marriage

After his first ship, David joined several others in succession over the following years eventually finding work on a hopper dredger in coastal waters.

He signed on this hopper dredger as second officer and earned a very good wage which included a freight bonus. The more trips the vessel made, the better was the bonus.

His contract on required him to serve onboard the vessel for twenty-one days and thereafter he would avail 7 days paid leave.

Whilst on leave after his third tour of duty he met Kathy. She worked as a barmaid in a club he used fairy often when in his hometown. She was very attractive with long auburn hair, hazel eyes that shined, around the same age, and fun to be with. They got on very well and after about seventeen months of courtship, David asked Kathy to marry him.

They married in church and honeymooned in Paris. David had accrued a reasonable amount of savings during his time in both the Merchant navy and in the dredging industry and was able to place a deposit on a 3-bedroom house in Windmill St, Gravesend.

At first, the marriage seemed to be perfect, by after just over two years, cracks began to appear. David noticed little things that indicated that Kathy was distancing herself from him.

She would be going out on "hen nights" quite often and arrive home in the early hours. She was never happy to speak to David about these nights out and he became suspicious.

Eventually, his suspicions were re-enforced when one of his close friends revealed that Kathy might be having a relationship with someone she worked with. On hearing this, David got angry with his friend and said he didn't believe him. But the seeds of suspicion were starting to develop.

One evening when Kathy was getting ready for a "hen night" with her friends, David followed her taxi. Her taxi headed for the General Gordon Hotel, and he parked his car and watched as she entered the hotel.

He stayed in his car for about ten minutes before entering the hotel lobby. The cocktail bar was just through the lounge and, keeping out of their sight, he could see Kathy sitting there with a man he recognised as the manager of the office where she worked.

David remained out of sight until about twenty minutes later they both left the bar and took the elevator to the second floor where the hotel rooms were housed. Obviously, they were having an affair.

He was devastated. He wanted to find our which room they were in and barge in to confront them. But he controlled the urge and waited in the lobby.

About four hours passed, the bar was closing. David went to his car and sat there. He was confused and didn't know what to do.

At around 11:30, Kathy appeared with her lover, and they went to where he had parked his car. They both got in and David followed. They drove in the direction of the home of David and Kathy, stopping at the end of the street.

David drove slowly approaching the parked car and stopping just behind it. He alighted.

The shock on Kathy's face was something to behold when David opened the passenger door.

"You bitch" he yelled. "You have been doing this for ages. WHY?"

The boyfriend cowered in his seat and David ran to his side preparing to pull him out and beat the hell out of him. But the boyfriend had locked his door. He then started the car engine, slammed it into gear and raced off down the street with Kathy inside.

David didn't follow this time. He went to his car and sat there for ten minutes contemplating what he was to do. He drove home and phoned the friend who had first told him about Kathy's infidelity.

His friend was sympathetic and offered to come over but David just wanted to be alone. He waited for Kathy until dawn, but she didn't arrive home.

The following morning David had to return to duty on the hopper dredger and during the day when the ship was berthed alongside the quay, David arranged for a relief officer to take his place for this trip only. He needed some time to himself.

Returning home in the early evening, he could see that Kathy had been there and had taken some of her clothes and jewellery and other personal items. Where she had gone he had no idea. She had not left a note.

Some days later, having not heard anything more from Kathy, David called her mothers house and Kathy answered the phone. She said she had made a huge mistake and was sorry. Would David have her back?

In truth, David still loved her but could not forgive her. She had broken his heart into a thousand pieces. He would never again be able to trust anyone like before. It was over…for good.

Kathy cried and begged for another chance, but David had made up his mind. He would file for divorce.

Kathy was represented at the court but did not contest the proceedings. David was eventually granted a divorce on the grounds of her adultery.

David began to drink increasingly, and his behaviour became unstable. He became unreliable and failed to turn up for duty on three occasions. He was eventually dismissed from his post.

He drifted for a while, moving to Jersey in the Channel Islands for a while. He even spent a few summer months living on the beach in Ostia just outside of Rome. He wandered Europe looking for something but not knowing what it was.

After returning to the UK , he found a job with Howard Marine Ltd. He was offered the position of Dredge-Master of a cutter suction dredger working on the new Felixstowe Port development. It was good money and offered secure employment for at least a couple of years. It was a new beginning.

Chapter 5 -Julie

Born in Camberwell London in 1935 to loving parents Arthur and Rosina Smith, Julie never had it easy as a child.

Four years later, her dad had gone off to fight the Germans, joining the Royal artillery and was then attached to the eighth army under Field Marshal Montgomery. He was to fight in many campaigns throughout 1939-45.

The family lived in a tenement building in Camberwell and when the second world began, Julie and her mum were evacuated to Radlett in Hertfordshire.

When they arrived at the allocated place where they were to stay in Radlett, they felt isolated and alone. They knew no-one here and the landlady was quite hostile towards them. She obviously resented the fact that she was providing four years old Julie and he mum with a temporary home away from the blitz.

They were provided with a meagre breakfast and a meal in the evening. Each morning after breakfast the woman of the house insisted they had to leave and return in late afternoon before the evening meal.

Julie and her mum had no choice and would spend the time walking around Radlett. It was often cold and damp and when it was raining they would take shelter in the bus shelter or in the park area where there was a huge oak tree just inside the gate.

One morning, it was raining heavily, and they sitting were on the bench under the oak tree. The local policeman came by on his bicycle and spoke to Rosina. He asked, "are you ok my dear".

Rosina told him they were waiting for five o'clock so they could go to the place where they were staying.

The policeman asked where that was and when Rosina gave him the address he looked away. Then he said. "Now you come along with me, you can't be out in this kind of weather".

He picked up Julie and placed her on the crossbar of his bicycle, and they walked together to where he lived.

It was a police house with a sign over the door, and they entered via the back garden gate and into the scullery of this large house. They were greeted warmly by Mrs. Fent, the policeman's wife. She got each of them a blanket and told Rosina that she had spare clothes she could use until her own had dried out.

She was kind and friendly and after saying something to Mr. Fent, he excused himself and left the house.

About 3 hours later, he came back with a small suitcase that Rosina recognised as her own.

Mr. Fent explained that he had spoken to the landlady of the place they were staying and insisted she pack all the belongings of Rosina and Julie. He said she would need to inform the authorities that Rosina and Julie were no longer staying there and would now be staying with the Fent family.

The Fents were just amazing and so friendly. Their eldest son was in the army and the two younger lads still in school. The huge back garden was full of vegetables, and they never went hungry. Rosina would help Mrs Fent in the kitchen and with the usual household chores.

They were very happy there together. And that is how it was for about 16 months until Grandad Charlie came and took them to another place to stay.

The place to stay was a two-bedroom cottage in Redbourn Herts. Julie was expecting to see her grandma and asked where she was. She was so looking forward to seeing her nana again after such a long time. She was just told that nana is no longer with us here in Redbourn.

It was much later, when Julie was about eight years old that she learned what really happened. Nana had been killed in London during a bombing raid.

Julie went to Redbourn infant/primary school until she was eleven and then on to Harpenden to a secondary modern girl's school.

Leaving school at 16, June started work at Suttons in Redbourn as a trainee seamstress. This developed further when she became fully qualified a few years later.

Julie met and married the son of a policeman and during this marriage she gave birth to three children.

But after their third child was born and had started school, June took up part time work as a barmaid in one of the local hospitality establishments. She enjoyed the work and it provided and additional outlet. The work would be a couple of evening a week and did not interfere with looking after her family.

Julie was a very attractive woman and would often get admiring glances from other men. But Julie was never the type of person who would betray her marriage vows of fidelity.

Her husband had been from the start quite possessive, but this never bothered June. although she had to be careful not to arouse unfounded jealousy when they were in the company of other people.

But since she had started this part time bar-work, his possessiveness transformed to bullying and abject jealousy.

It was now beginning to affect Julie very much and his bullying turned to violence. He would start accusing her of flirting when there was absolutely no justification. This could turn to him attacking her physically. More than once, she ended up with bruising on her body and sometimes had a black eye from his aggressive bullying behaviour.

It reached a point when after he had tried to strangle her, she had no choice but to pack a bag, leave the house. She booked into a bed and breakfast place. She called her daughter and told her where she was. Her husband came and begged her to come back after promising it would never happen again. And so, she thought of the kids and everything else and was prepared to give it one more go.

But again, he just a couple of days later, he was up to his old tricks and again became aggressive. Whilst she had gone with her friend to the school to pick up her eldest boy, her husband appeared. He grabbed her by the hair and made her get into his own car. On the way, as he was forced to slow right down at the bottom of the street, Julie opened the door and leaped out.

Someone across the road called to Julie. Julie crossed the road to this woman who aid she saw her jump from the car. Julie asked her to help, and the woman helped her into the car and took her to the school to collect her son. As soon as her son saw her he noticed the blood on her head and cried out *"Mum, mum, there's blood".* This was where her husband had forced her into his car a few minutes earlier.

The kindly woman asked Julie if she should take her to the hospital, but Julie asked her instead to take her to her mum and dads' home in Redbourn.

Arriving home mum was shocked to see her condition and provided a little first aid to where the hair had been yanked from her head leaving a bloody wound.

Her dad arrived soon after as Rosina had called him at his work just down the road.

As soon as Arthur saw Julie he was furious. *"Did he do this to you? I'll bloody kill the bastard."*

Her son, sitting there in bewilderment at all the trauma looked at his mum and went over for a cuddle. It was so painful for everyone.

Sometime later, after taking legal advice, Julie started divorce proceedings.

She stayed with her mum and dad and kept in touch whenever possible with her other two children still living with their father. Her eldest son stayed with her at her parents' house.

In July 1972, Julie and her friend Maggie hired a caravan on a site at Felixstowe in Suffolk. With her eldest son now ten years old plus Maggie and two of her own young children, they planned to spend at least a week in Felixstowe and enjoy the benefits this lovely little town had to offer.

On the second day they were there, they had a problem with the door lock on their rental caravan. Whilst they were trying to resolve the problem, a fellow in the opposite caravan, called out and asked if they needed a hand.

He came over and introduced himself. *"I'm David, I am working on the new Port project. Let's have a look at this."*

And so began the love story of his life and perhaps of Julie too.

Chapter 6 – The locksmith

David collected a screwdriver from his toolbox in the caravan and set about removing the faulty lock. A part inside had broken and was not repairable. And so, David fetched a new lock from the local hardware store and fixed it. This being done, he was offered a cup of coffee and so it began.

The children were playing in the children's play area close by and the three adults sat together outside the caravan in the warm summer sunshine. It was peaceful and so relaxing.

There was an instant and mutual attraction between David and Julie. Maggie noticed it too and made an excuse to go over to see the children so that David and Julie were left on their own for a while.

They chatted freely and Julie told David about her divorce proceedings and the children. She wanted to be open and honest from the start. David too told her about Kathy and the breakdown of the marriage. They had a lot in common.

It was a weekend off work for David and so he asked Julie if he could take her out for a meal that evening. She agreed. That evening, David called on Julie and they walked the short distance into the town where David had booked a table at the Poppies restaurant.

They enjoyed a nice meal, and David ordered a bottle of wine. Julie declined the offer of a glass of wine saying he preferred a "pineapple juice".

After the meal came coffee. David tried to persuade Julie to try one of the special "Gaelic Coffee Specials" that Poppies restaurant was renowned for. But again, Julie declined settling instead for a cup of tea.

After the meal David took her to a pub that he used frequently. He was obviously well known in the pub as all the bar staff greeted him by name as did several of the customers in the bar. David seemed to be able to drink quite a lot of beer (draft Guinness particularly) which would be interspersed with shots of whisky.

Julies Dad liked a pint or two and her mum Rosina was partial to a glass or two of the old "amber nectar," so Julie was not fussed by the amount of alcohol David was drinking.

After a lovely evening together, David took Julie back to her caravan and they arranged to see each other again the following day.

The weekend over, David went back to his duties on the project. He worked twelve hour shifts offshore on a cutter suction dredger and including travel to and from the vessel by boat at the start and finish of each shift, his work consumed the best part of fourteen hours each day.

His contract was for 14 consecutive days work and then a "long weekend" of three days. These days off would not always coincide with the traditional Saturday and Sunday weekend, but this was the pattern of his schedule.

Julie and her son Mark, who David had got to know during the week, prepared to leave the park on the Friday morning to head back to Redbourn. They knocked on the door of Davids caravan and said goodbye. But before they left, David and Julie arranged to meet when his next "long weekend" was due.

Trafalgar Square

It was a warm morning two weeks later when David caught the train from Ipswich into London. Crossing over by bus from St Pancras Station he arrived at Trafalgar square. He made his way to the side of the square adjacent to the National Art Gallery and waited.

The arrangement was to meet at 10:30 and he was early. That was his maritime training kicking in. Never be late on duty, - a cardinal sin in the Merchant Navy.

Looking around the square with many tourists and visitors from far and wide, he spotted a beautiful woman wearing a short white pleated skirt with a navy-blue top. Her long legs sheathed in sheer black stockings. It was Julie. She had not yet seen him. He waved but she still did not see him.

He approached the place she was standing. She had turned away from the direction he came from and was looking around when he crept up behind her and tapped he on the shoulder.

She spun around and when she saw him greeted him with that wonderful, beautiful smile he had grown to love.

They had no plans about what they might do today and so they went across to the café inside the National Art Gallery where they enjoyed a light breakfast.

Julie said to David that she had told her mum about him and was going to meet him in London. Her mum was pleased she had found someone she liked to be with again as the divorce proceedings were so stressful and she no longer wanted to trust anyone. David understood this too and had in fact written a letter and told his own mum about Julie.

Leaving the art gallery, they made their way to Leicester Square and then on to Soho to explore the sights and sounds of this bustling city. David discovered that the train back to Redbourn was not until 6:50 that evening and so they had plenty of time to see more of the sights. At the end of the afternoon, they both went over to Victoria railway station so that Julie could get the 6:50 train. This would take her to St Albans station, from where she would get a bus to Redbourn. They promised to stay in touch by phone and mail until the next time they could meet.

Two months later, David lost his job. He had no-one to blame but himself. He was dismissed for drinking alcohol whilst on the job. He had taken a bottle of whisky to the dredger one morning and had finished almost half the bottle by mid-day. Unfortunately for him, the project Superintendent paid an unscheduled visit to the dredger soon after twelve o'clock. He spoke to David and noticed he'd been drinking. David had failed to conceal the bottle, and it was discovered. An altercation followed with the Superintendent calling ashore for a replacement crew member and David was given a verbal notice of dismissal there and then for gross misconduct.

He packed up his belongings from his cabin and was taken ashore. Later that afternoon, a letter of dismissal was issued to him. And that was that. Another good job lost because of his drinking pattern. Perhaps he should try to do something about it.

He had arranged with Julie that she would visit him at Felixstowe and stay with him in his caravan during his next "long weekend". They had become closer and were planning to set up home together. David had found a lovely apartment in Felixstowe and had agreed with the owner to rent it for twelve months. This was all arranged before he lost his job. He had already written to Julie about the apartment, but when she arrived at his caravan in Felixstowe, she hadn't expected his first words to be, *"I lost my job."*

He told her the truth and explained that he planned to cut back on his drinking. Julie didn't seem troubled by any of it.

She simply replied, *"Don't worry, you'll soon find aner one. In the meantime, I'll find a job, we'll manage."*

The next day, Julie, Mark, and David all moved into the apartment at The Undercliff. It was a beautiful place, built into the cliffside with wonderful views overlooking the promenade and the wide sweep of the North Sea.

They arranged for Mark to attend a local primary school which luckily was just five minutes' walk from the apartment. In no time at all, Julie had found a little job that fitted in with allowing her to take Mark to and from school. He soon seemed to settle in.

About two weeks after they had moved into to The Undercliff, a fellow that David had worked with on the Ports project told him that Mike Stone, the Managing Director of Cunis Delta - a dredging company, would like David to call his secretary as he had a possible job for him.

David called the number he'd been given and spoke to the secretary of Mike Stone. She asked if he would like to come to their offices in Essex to meet her boss Mike.

And so, a couple of days later, David was sitting in the office of Mike Stone, a huge fellow who had a good reputation in the Dredging and Marine Construction sector.

After the usual formalities, Mike asked David about his career to date and David filled him in . Mike finally asked David WHY he had left Howard Marine Ltd at Felixstowe.

David just told him plainly and without making any excuses, " I let them down by drinking on the job and was sacked for gross misconduct".

Mike was silent for a minute and David thought to himself, that the interview was over.

He was about to get up from his chair to leave when Mike Stone said.

"I appreciate your honesty. I already knew why you had left. I just wanted to meet you as I was told you are pretty good at your work. Do you think you can handle a job in the North of Scotland for me? We are dredging a channel for a new oil related project and it's running late. I want someone to get involved to turn things around and I think that someone might just be you David."

With that, Mike laid out more details of the project and asked David if he was the right man for the job.

"Yes, I'm your man, and I won't let you down" David replied. They shook hands on it and David went through to see the secretary.

Before he left the office, David was handed reimbursement for his travel expenses and informed that a ticket would be waiting for him the next day at the Dan Air desk in Heathrow's Terminal One, ready for his flight to Dalcross Airport in Inverness-shire.

When he returned to The Undercliff, Julie and Mark were delighted to see David in such high spirits. Julie wasn't thrilled about him flying off for a new job the next day, but with a schedule of two weeks on and one week off, she knew it would be manageable. After all, this was only the beginning of their new life together.

Ardersier

The flight from Heathrow took a little under two hours and was uneventful. The food was very good, and the drinks were free on the old Dakota aircraft.

Coming out of the baggage are David saw a man holding a small board with is name on it. David approached him and introduced himself to "Fergie", an employee of Cunis Delta and now Davids new employer.

Fergie told David he had been instructed by the project manager to take him to a hotel in the nearby town of Nairn where he would stay overnight. Fergie would then come back for him the following morning to take David to the project offices.

The hotel was a bit drab and after placing his gear in the allocated room, David went out to explore the town. It was just after eight pm and the streets seemed uninteresting in the Autumn evening. He walked through the High Street and went into a pub on a corner. He ordered a drink and went over to the end of the bar where there were a couple of vacant bar stools.

A fellow standing nearby gave him a nod, and David greeted him. They began chatting, and the man said something along the lines of, "Och, you're English, eh?"

"I hope that's not a problem," David joked. "It's been over two hundred years since the Battle of Culloden, after all."

That was David's first lesson about being an Englishman in the Highlands of Scotland: don't mention Culloden—especially if you're English. It can spark arguments you never intended to have.

Before long, others in the bar joined in, and a discussion erupted about the Jacobite rebellion and the long, troubled history between England and Scotland. The atmosphere grew increasingly heated, particularly when David offered his own opinion. He soon realised that prejudice was outweighing reason, and he wisely excused himself, saying he had to meet a friend back at the hotel.

The following morning after taking a shower David enjoyed a very nice breakfast in the hotel restaurant. At around nine am, Fergie arrived in the minibus and took David to meet Frank Bedingfield, the project manager. Frank was amiable and together they talked about Davids previous marine experiences and the project in hand.

Frank explained that the contract entailed dredging a channel from the deeper waters of the Moray firth to a designated area onshore. The dredged materials would be pumped ashore, and the reclaimed land would be the future construction facility for oil rig jackets and associated platform support systems.

The two main items of equipment were two cutter-suction dredgers. These were supported offshore by a hydrographic survey vessel, two tugboats and two workboats.

The crews consisted of dredge operators, boat skippers, deckhands, welders and other associated personnel.

On shore a team of people were located and led by Dougie Fraser who was the fill-master responsible for the development of the fill area and the overall functioning of the workshop.

There were two surveyors and one site engineer based in the site offices, along with the project manager.

Frank explained to David that there were three primary reasons that had been identified for the delays.

- Inclement weather and rough seas.
- Breakdowns of the marine equipment.
- Kelp on the seabed.

It was up to David to find a solution for each of these items and as soon as possible. The client, McDermott an American company was threatening to enforce contractual liquidated damages penalties if progress was not improved significantly, and soon.

After a tour of the vessels accompanied by Frank and after being introduced to the senior operators and other players in the project, David, always up for a challenge, set about his task.

His strategy initially began to first spend a little time onboard the two dredgers to assess the behaviour, disciplines, skills, efforts of the primary players. He worked long hours each day, sometimes up to eighteen, so that he could cover at least a part of both the day shift and night shift on each of the two dredgers. Almost right away, he saw that the dredge operators without exception were lacking. Here was the first problem. It had to be resolved.

He raised these concerns immediately with Frank and urged him to speak to Mike Stone to recruit at least two experienced and industrious dredge operators, even if he had to bring them in from Holland.

The next thing was the damages created during inclement weather, mainly to the floating pipelines. David gave clear instructions that weather forecasts must be noted every day throughout the day by the site office and this information relayed to all offshore vessels. In case of any projected winds over 20 knots, the pipelines were to be disconnected and beached safely until the sea conditions became suitable to commence work. These procedures had to be strictly followed for the duration of the project.

The seabed was covered in heavy kelp which clogged the suction intake. This meant that after just a few minutes of dredging, the dredging operation was halted to allow the cutter ladder to be raised and the cutter cleared of kelp. Then the ladder was lowered again to the seabed level and dredging would again commence.

A detailed study of the dredging logs during the several months before he arrived, David could see that losses incurred due to the cutter being clogged with kelp amounted to over sixty percent of operational time. This was outrageous. Why had this not been taken seriously prior to his arrival. Why had it been allowed to continue.

David went to see a local farmer and sought his advice on which type of plough would be able to gather kelp from the seabed and drag it to one side of the pre dredged area of the seabed and release it to be gathered by a clamshell.

After listening to the advice David himself sat at the drawing board for several hours and designed a plough. He kept the workshop operating day and night fabricate the plough.

It was completed in three days and trials started by attaching a bridle to a wire rope and attaching it to one of the workboats which was fitted with a 5 tonne Hyab crane.

It took a couple more days to adjust and to clear an area close to the last dredged position. And it was such a relief when the experiment produced results. David sent the divers down to check the are and they reported back that the area was not entirely cleared of the kelp but almost ninety percent had been dragged to the side of the cut.

Now one of the onshore excavators was rigged with a clamshell attachment and the unit loaded onto a 36-metre flat top barge. It proved successful.

After ten days assessment it showed that the downtime for cutter cleaning had come down from around sixty percent to less than five percent. This was a real success.

Meanwhile, two new recruits were sent from head office for evaluation. Both were from Holland and were fluent in spoken and written English. They quickly became influential in improving the performance of the dredging operations.

After a month, two of the original operators—deemed liabilities—were given their notice. This had a motivating effect on the rest of the team, and within five months of David's involvement, Mike Stone visited the site and took him to lunch at the King's Kitchen in Elgin.

During lunch, Mike handed David an envelope containing a substantial ex gratia payment for his work. He then asked whether David would be willing to take over from Frank as project manager, as Frank was needed for a new project starting in Dorset.

David agreed to the proposed terms and conditions but explained that he would need to be available full-time, meaning he would have to bring Julie and Mark to Scotland. Mike told him to make whatever arrangements were necessary and assured him that the company would cover accommodation and transport costs where appropriate.

David presented the plan to Julie and Mark, and they began preparing to leave The Undercliff.

But then came the bombshell.

Whilst Mark was on a scheduled week-long visit to stay with his brother and sister, his father—upon learning of the impending move to Scotland, obtained a court order preventing Mark from leaving England. His lawyer cited differences in the legal systems which enabled his father to secure a temporary restraint.

Julie knew of course that her ex-husband was using the child as leverage and he was determined to make Julie look as though she was not a fit mother. He claimed that Mark would be better off with his elder sister and younger brother in the family home with their father and filed for custody.

I addition, he refused to allow Mark to return to Felixstowe and now began a protracted legal tussle which would go on and on.

After a long tussle, it was decided by the divorce court that the father would retain custody of all three children in the (former) matrimonial home in St. Albans and Julie would have visiting rights.

Chapter 7 – From UK to Kuwait

Arriving in Dalcross airport on a very cold and wintry evening Julie and David made their way to a guest house that had been arranged for them to stay whilst they found more permanent accommodation for themselves.

Their new chapter in Scotland began humbly, in a rented caravan in the village of Ardersier. It was cramped and temporary, but it was theirs—for a while. Eventually, they were offered the chance to rent a small two-bedroom house in the same village, and for the first time in a long time, life felt as though it was beginning to settle into something hopeful.

Julie was pregnant by then, and in May 1975 she gave birth to a son. They named him **Scott**, after the boy of a family who had become dear friends. With the new baby and a comfortable home, it seemed they had finally found their place. Happiness, for once, felt secure.

But stability in the Highlands was short-lived. When the dredging project ended, David was forced to move on, taking work in Kishorn on the massive construction of the Ninian Field platform in the North Sea. The job was demanding, the hours long, and the pressure constant.

Then came the blow he never saw coming—David's mother passed away. The loss struck deeply, and with heavy hearts he, Julie, and little Scott left Scotland behind, returning to Kent to live with David's father.

The England they returned to was in turmoil. The 1970s were years riddled with industrial unrest—strikes sweeping the whole nation, industries grinding to a halt, and work becoming painfully scarce. David eventually secured a job at the Littlebrook Power Station in Greenhithe, and for a moment, life steadied.

But the tension inside the house was building. The relationship between David's father and Julie deteriorated rapidly, reaching a breaking point from which there was no return. Forced to escape the conflict, David and Julie moved with Scott to the Isle of Grain, hoping for peace and a fresh start.

Instead, the strikes tightened their grip on the country, dragging the family deeper into financial struggle. Day after day, David felt the weight of failure pressing harder on his shoulders—the gnawing despair of a man who could not provide the life he wanted for those he loved.

At last, worn down and demoralised, he made a painful decision. If he couldn't find a future in England, he would have to seek one elsewhere. And so, he began looking for work overseas, driven not by ambition, but by necessity—and by the fierce need to give his family something better than the life that was slipping through his fingers.

A friend from David's hopper-dredger days, a man named **Mike Harding**, had long since moved on to a well-placed position in a company in Kuwait.

When Mike returned to the UK for a short leave, he and David met up for a few drinks—just like old times.

Over pints and familiar stories, Mike revealed that his company was actively searching for experienced UK dredging personnel. Mike told David that he would fit the bill perfectly.

Before they parted, Mike handed him the company's details and the name of the Personnel Manager, insisting he should apply.

The very next day, David called Kuwait. They asked him to send his career details, so he faxed his CV along with a covering letter—and waited.

Two days later he received a telephone call from Mr. Abdul Ridha Juma the company Personnel Manager.

A week later, an envelope arrived. Inside was an employment letter and a contract offering a three-month probationary period, with the possibility of a full two-year contract if all went well.

David and Julie went over the details and discussed the pros and cons in depth. Accepting meant he wouldn't see Julie or little Scott for three long months. But the offer was substantial—and tax-free. It was the kind of opportunity that could change their future. In the end, they agreed: he had to take it.

Two weeks later, David stood in Heathrow Airport, ticket in hand, boarding a British Airways flight bound for Kuwait.

The plane touched down at Kuwait Airport at 18:45. David had been assured that someone from the company would meet him upon arrival. But after clearing immigration and waiting almost an hour, it became clear—no one was coming.

So, he decided to step outside into the heavy desert air, where he flagged down a taxi and asked to be taken to a hotel in the city. The driver took him to the Hilton on the Corniche, where David booked a room for the night.

Sleep did not come easily. At around 5:00 a.m., he was startled awake by haunting voices drifting from several nearby minarets—the call to prayer echoing across the still-dark city. It was his first true reminder that he was far from home.

Later that morning, he went down for breakfast and phoned the company office. This time, a car was promptly dispatched to collect him. It drove him to their headquarters on Khalid Bin Walid Street, where he finally met the Personnel Manager and the Managing Director.

That afternoon, David was taken to a building in Fintas, a small coastal town south of Kuwait City. He was given a furnished bedroom and introduced to the housekeeper who oversaw the property. This would be his home throughout the three-month probationary period. Meals were provided, laundry was taken care of, and two company saloon cars were available for personal use. David was free to take either one, using his UK driving licence until he could obtain a Kuwaiti one.

The next morning, he boarded a crew bus with several other employees and headed to **Shuaiba**, where a major port-extension project was underway. From there, he was taken offshore to a massive cutter-suction dredger—one of the most powerful in the world at the time. Built in Holland, the vessel stretched almost ninety metres in length with a beam of eighteen metres.

David's post was **Second Dredgemaster**, reporting directly to the captain, a Dutchman named **Henk Guntlisbergen**.

The crew consisted of sixty-four men, working two twelve-hour shifts. Nearly all senior roles—except David's—were held by Dutch personnel. The deckhands came from Singapore, the engine-room crew were mostly Dutch, surveyors were Singaporean, welders and greasers were Pakistani, and the cooks hailed from Somalia.

It didn't take long for David to sense the atmosphere around him. Although company policy stated that Dutch crewmembers would eventually be replaced by British staff, there was a quiet, unmistakable hostility beneath the surface. It was subtle—never openly stated—but he could feel it. And soon he realised that he was being assigned the most difficult operational tasks, long before they were handed to any of the Dutch crew.

But David was stubborn—unyieldingly so. Despite their efforts to trip him up or make him appear out of his depth, he refused to fail. With each challenge, he grew more confident.

And then came an unexpected turn: **Captain Henk**, who seemed to be the least prejudiced among the Dutch officers, began sending back excellent reports on David's progress and performance. His evaluations cut straight through the quiet resistance aboard the vessel.

Even so, the company's leadership in Kuwait—the Works Manager, Marine Superintendent, and Fill-Master—were all Dutch as well. The hierarchy was firmly rooted, and David remained the outsider pushing his way in.

When David's three-month probationary period ended, he was instructed to report to the head office in Kuwait City. He was interviewed first by **Mr. Jumah**, and shortly afterward he found himself seated in the office of **Mr. Fadel Abu Abbas**, the Managing Director.

Mr. Fadel greeted him warmly. Then, with a smile that carried both confidence and approval, he told David he would be pleased to offer him a **two-year contract on married status**. The offer was generous: a promotion to **First Dredgemaster** with a higher salary, western-standard married accommodation, a private car for his exclusive use, and annual family air tickets to and from the UK.

David was both surprised and impressed. Before accepting, he asked if he could telephone Julie in England to see whether she would be willing to bring Scott and start a new life in Kuwait.

Before going on leave, David accepted the accommodation the company had found for him and Julie located in the town of Fahaheel.

And so, it came to pass that David, Julie, and young Scott stood on the brink of yet another adventure—one that would shape their lives in ways they could not yet imagine.

A few days later, David was back in England with Julie and Scott, and together they began preparing for their new life in Kuwait. They agreed to keep their house in Kent for the time being—just in case. It felt safer not to let it out until they knew how their future abroad would unfold.

When they finally arrived in Kuwait, Julie experienced a genuine culture shock. Everything—the heat, the sounds, the pace of life—felt so different from anything she had known. Scott, on the other hand, adapted instantly. People were charmed by the little English boy, and he quickly became the centre of friendly attention wherever they went.

Their new apartment was spacious beyond anything they had expected: three bedrooms, a large living room, a full kitchen, a bathroom, and a balcony overlooking the bustling fish market and the harbour below.

Julie would walk with Scott to the markets in the nearby streets and was amazed at how friendly the shopkeepers were. If she saw something she liked for Scott and the shopkeeper did not have the right size or colour, he would send one of the assistants scurrying off to return in a few minutes with something suitable. Of course there would also be the offer of "chai", the customary cup of weak sweet black tea found everywhere in the middle east region. All part of the Arabian hospitality. Just wonderful.

David would be working most days and would be away from the apartment for up to 15 hours every day. But at least they were together full time now.

Living in Kuwait at that time was an experience unlike any other.

Kuwait was booming—oil wealth was transforming the country at a breathtaking pace. The streets were busy with expatriates from all over the world: engineers, teachers, contractors, doctors, and workers from Asia, Africa, and Europe. The city felt like a crossroads of cultures.

The days were hot—scorchingly so in summer. By mid-afternoon the heat could be fierce enough to make the horizon shimmer. Air conditioning wasn't a luxury; it was a necessity. Yet the evenings carried a kind of magic. Families strolled along the Corniche, the sea breeze offering a welcome relief from the day's intensity. The scent of roasted nuts, grilled kebabs, and cardamom tea drifted from market stalls, mixing with the sound of distant laughter and lively conversation.

Shopping was an adventure. In the souks, merchants called out from behind stacked displays of spices, rugs, gold jewellery, and fresh produce. Haggling was expected and almost playful—a dance of smiles, raised eyebrows, and theatrical sighs. Julie found herself gradually learning the rhythm of it.

Expat life had its own community, too. Western-style supermarkets were emerging. Social clubs and gatherings helped newcomers find their footing. Women from many nations formed friendships that crossed cultural lines, bonded by the shared challenge of building a life far from home.

But it wasn't without difficulties. The cultural differences were sometimes startling. The conservative dress of local women, the call to prayer echoing from the mosques five times a day, the strict laws, and the absence of some freedoms taken for granted in England—it all required adjustment. Yet there was a warmth in the people, a sense of safety, and a generosity that often surprised them. For

David, Kuwait meant opportunity, responsibility, and the promise of a stable future. For Julie and Scott, it meant discovery—new sights, new customs, new friends, and a vastly different way of life.

In 1979, Scott was enrolled at **The Kuwait English School** in Fahaheel. The headmistress, **Miss William (OBE)**, was from Wales, and Scott immediately loved the school. Many of the teachers were British, and the building was only a short walk from their apartment, which made the mornings easy and familiar.

Julie soon got to know several Japanese ladies who lived in the same building, and she formed a particularly close friendship with **Mrs. Sase**, the wife of the Managing Director of Mitsui Engineering in Kuwait. Mrs. Sase became very fond of Scott; she doted on him and would bring him little gifts each time she saw him, always smiling as though he were one of her own.

On the rare occasions when David had a day off, the three of them treasured the time together. They loved going early in the morning to the quiet, uncrowded beach where the warm, azure waters of the Arabian Gulf shimmered under the rising sun.

After a leisurely swim, they would head home to shower and dress, then drive into Kuwait City for lunch at the Sheraton Hotel's rooftop restaurant. From there, the view over the city and along the Corniche was breathtaking—an endless sweep of coastline, shimmering sea, and sunlit buildings that made them feel, just for a moment, as though the whole world lay open before them.

Kuwait, being an Islamic state, did not permit the consumption of alcohol anywhere in the country. Embassies, of course, served it privately, but there were no bars, no liquor stores, and no legal way for the public to purchase it.

This led many expatriates—especially those from Western countries—to make their own homemade "hooch."

The process was surprisingly simple. A 60-litre plastic barrel could be bought in the local market, along with bottles of grape juice. Sugar and yeast were cheap and plentiful. With those ingredients, anyone inclined could produce their own rough but drinkable wine.

David learned the method from another Western colleague and was soon brewing his own personal supply. For many expatriates, social life revolved around gatherings in each other's homes, where homemade wine appeared quietly on tables, or (very discreetly), around dinners in hotel restaurants to celebrate birthdays and special occasions.

Scott, meanwhile, had a full range of after-school activities to choose from— Taekwondo sessions, playtimes with friends, and gatherings with children from the neighbourhood. Julie's social life also flourished. She formed friendships with people from a remarkable mix of cultures and nationalities, creating a network that helped Kuwait feel more like home.

One of the great advantages of living in Kuwait at that time was the sense of safety. Women, children—indeed, almost everyone—could walk freely and confidently through most areas of the country, day or night.

Shopping offered its own blend of modern and traditional. The new air-conditioned malls were sophisticated, bright, and filled with international goods, while the older souks were lively and atmospheric, full of spices, fabrics, perfumes, jewellery, and hand-crafted items. Many things were far less expensive than similar goods back in the UK, making shopping both enjoyable and affordable.

Chapter 8 – New House

In 1984, during a holiday spent visiting friends, David and Julie decided to buy a brand-new three-bedroom house in Inverness, Scotland. They both held warm memories of their earlier years in the Highlands, and during this visit they toured a new development on the west bank of the Caledonian Canal. One particular property, the show-house, captured their hearts immediately. It was beautifully furnished, tastefully decorated, and felt like a place they could happily return to. They bought it exactly as seen, fittings and furnishings included.

The house in the Isle of Grain had been sold earlier in the year, and the proceeds went toward the deposit. They agreed that it would be beneficial for Scott, who would soon be eleven, to continue his education in Scotland. The new Inverness home would serve as a stepping stone toward that future.

Because it was Scott's summer break from school, Julie and Scott stayed in Scotland for several weeks while David flew back to Kuwait for work. They joined him again the following month.

On **May 25, 1985**, Kuwait was shaken by a dramatic assassination attempt on Emir **Sheikh Jaber Al-Ahmad Al-Sabah**. A suicide car bomber targeted his motorcade, narrowly missing the Emir. The attack was quickly attributed to pro-Iranian extremist groups—a conclusion that made sense, given Kuwait's visible support for Iraq since the Iran–Iraq war had begun five years earlier.

Kuwait had been supplying Iraq with logistical assistance, and its port at **Shuaiba** had become a crucial transit hub for weapons and military supplies purchased by Kuwait and forwarded to Iraq. Throughout this period, ships frequently berthed at Shuaiba carrying tanks, artillery, ammunition, trucks—military cargo sourced from the UK, the USA, and other suppliers.

Night after night, long convoys of trucks rumbled north along **Highway 80** toward the Abdali border crossing before disappearing into Iraq, their destinations undisclosed. The region was tense, heavily watched, and always humming with activity.

David happened to be managing a project close to the site of the assassination attempt. In the aftermath, security in the entire area tightened dramatically, and progress on the project was hindered by constant checks, restrictions, and the heightened presence of armed patrols.

The Offshore Preservation Project

The offshore project David was managing, though modest in scale compared to the vast dredging works he had overseen in previous years, carried a unique prestige. It was not merely a construction job—it was an attempt to preserve a piece of Kuwait's industrial heritage.

The structure lay just one kilometre off the coast, standing alone in the shallow waters of the Gulf. It was a squat, weathered platform—simple in design, almost crude by modern standards—but it held immense historical value: **it marked the site of the very first offshore oil well ever drilled in Kuwait**, decades earlier, during the early years of the country's oil exploration boom.

When David first visited the site, the platform showed its age. The steel legs were pitted and scarred with corrosion from decades of exposure to saltwater. The deck plates rattled underfoot, and the small work sheds were discoloured by sun and storms. Much of the equipment had been removed long ago, leaving rusted anchor points and obsolete fixtures behind.

The company did not tender for the project. Instead, because the company was now a wholly owned and operated Kuwaiti company, the client, the government of Kuwait, insisted that Kuwait Maritime & Dredging Co. - (KMD), the company David worked for, be awarded the contract on an agreed "cost plus" basis.

The task before him was to *"restore the platform to safe, presentable condition without altering the authenticity of its original structure, all in accordance with the very detailed specifications as outlined in the contract documents."*

This meant a careful balance of engineering precision and historical sensitivity. Modern methods couldn't simply be forced upon an outdated layout; the work had to be adapted, adjusted, reshaped to fit the limitations of a platform designed in another era.

Daily Operations

Every morning, David and his team set out on a company launch from Shuaiba harbour. The journey to the platform took around thirty minutes, depending on the tides and the state of the sea. Some days the Gulf was glassy and calm, reflecting the sun in dazzling silver sheets; other days it heaved and rolled, forcing the crew to cling to railings and gear as the boat pitched beneath them.

Once aboard the platform, the work was demanding but rewarding:

- Corroded beams were stripped and reinforced with new steel plates.

- Sections of the deck were removed and replaced, one panel at a time, ensuring the original dimensions were preserved.

- Protective coatings were applied in stages, with careful attention to the extreme heat, which cured paint too quickly and sometimes unevenly.

- The old support braces beneath the platform—twisted and worn—were realigned and stabilised using underwater welding teams brought in from Dubai.

The workers assigned to the project came from a variety of nationalities: Filipino scaffolders, Pakistani welders, Indian riggers, and a small supervisory team of Europeans. Despite language barriers, they operated with a quiet rhythm, each man knowing his task and carrying it out with disciplined precision.

Although it was a small project in terms of manpower and cost, the Ministry of Oil who was overseeing the project, took a keen interest in its progress. Senior officials visited periodically, arriving by helicopter to inspect the site. They viewed the platform not as an industrial relic, but as a symbol of Kuwait's early ambitions—its first steps toward becoming one of the world's major oil producers.

This meant that mistakes were not an option. David felt the weight of responsibility every day. The assassination attempt on the Emir had already heightened tensions throughout the country, and security at offshore sites was now stricter than ever. Armed patrol boats sometimes idled nearby, watching the crew as they worked.

Yet despite the pressure, the project advanced steadily. David's reputation for delivering results, even under difficult circumstances, became increasingly recognised by both the company and the Kuwaiti officials overseeing the restoration.

In quieter moments, David would stand at the railing, looking back toward the faint outline of the coastline. The platform creaked softly beneath him, a relic of another time.

He often imagined the original drilling crew working here decades earlier—men from faraway countries, sweating under the same sun, battling the same sea, never knowing the enormous wealth their efforts would one day unleash.

Restoring the platform felt, in some small way, like honouring their labour.

Despite the security delays which were frequent and disruptive, the project was completed, although several weeks beyond the initially projected time scale. But a completion certificate was issued by the client representative, the retention money returned and full payment received for the project.

Bill Meeks

David first met **William "Bill" Meeks** in 1987 while working on the refurbishment of the Small Boat Harbour in **Mina Al Ahmadi**—a demanding project commissioned by Kuwait Oil Company. The work was extensive: demolishing the old piers that had served the harbour for decades, dredging both the basin and the approach channel, and constructing a new marina capable of berthing thirty service vessels, each up to fifteen metres long. It was a meticulous, high-pressure job—made even more so by the constant oversight of the American engineering firm **Parsons**, hired to supervise every aspect of the project.

At the helm of Parsons' team was Bill Meeks.

Bill was not the kind of man one forgot easily. He carried himself with the quiet confidence of someone who had lived through things most men never would. An ex-U.S. Navy SEAL, he had served in some of the world's harshest environments before leaving the military to start his own commercial diving company in Texas. His firm specialised in underwater operations for major oil companies such as Chevron—pipeline inspections, deep-water welding, salvage work, and everything in between.

By the time David met him, Bill had already sold the company, securing enough financial comfort to choose only the projects that interested him. But despite his success, there was nothing boastful about him. He spoke with the easy calm of a man who had nothing left to prove.

David remembered their first conversation vividly. Bill stood on the dock, boots planted wide, arms folded, observing the demolition crew with a scrutiny so sharp it felt almost physical. His sun-weathered face, partly hidden beneath a Navy ballcap, betrayed no emotion—no approval, no irritation—just a level, calculating interest in everything happening around him.

When he finally turned to David, his handshake was firm, his voice low and steady.

"Bill Meeks," he said. "Parson's oversight. You must be the man running the dredging side."

David nodded and introduced himself, already sensing that this was someone he could respect.

Over the following weeks, they developed a professional rapport that quickly grew into genuine camaraderie. Bill had a wealth of stories from his years as a SEAL—stories he rarely shared, and only when he trusted the listener. More often, he spoke about the diving operations he'd run, the technical challenges he'd faced, and the strange, sometimes dangerous situations offshore work could create. He had a dry humour too—subtle, occasionally dark, but always disarming.

What impressed David most was Bill's leadership. He was demanding, yes, but never unreasonable. He expected excellence from everyone because he lived by the same standard. When problems arose—and in a project involving demolition, dredging, and marine construction, they inevitably did—Bill approached each one like a tactical puzzle, breaking it down with military precision.

The incident happened late one afternoon, when the heat still rippled off the concrete piers and the harbour water glimmered like molten glass. The demolition crew had been working for hours removing one of the old piers—an ageing concrete structure weakened by decades of saltwater and fuel spills. Everything had gone according to plan until a sudden, sharp crack split the air.

David looked up instantly. A section of the pier—far larger than predicted—had sheared loose beneath the jackhammer team. Instead of collapsing straight down as the structural survey suggested it would, the slab twisted sideways, sliding dangerously toward the edge of the work platform. Beneath it, several labourers were still positioning cables for the crane lift.

David shouted for the men to clear the area, but the noise of machinery drowned him out.

Bill reacted first.

He moved with astonishing speed for a man his age—faster than anyone would expect from someone with his calm demeanour. He sprinted across the platform, waving both arms and bellowing with a voice trained to command attention in combat zones. The workers finally heard him and scrambled clear just as the huge, fractured slab teetered on its edge.

But it wasn't over. One of the support beams holding the slab had buckled, and a cascade of smaller fragments threatened to break free and tumble into the harbour—right where the survey boat and its crew were stationed.

David reached the control stand of the crane and shouted to the operator through the headset.

"Drop the boom ten metres—slowly! Get that sling tight before the whole thing goes!"

The operator hesitated. The angles were wrong. The load unstable. One mistake and the crane could topple.

Bill reached the cabin a moment later, leaning in with the same unshakeable authority. "Do it. Now. Follow his call."

The operator swallowed, nodded, and began lowering the boom. Sweat trickled down his forehead despite the air-conditioned cabin. David calculated distances in his head, adjusting the commands by instinct rather than mathematics.

"Two metres… one… hold it!"

The sling caught the edge of the slab just as it began to slide again.

"Lift—slow!" David barked.

The crane groaned under the strain, but the slab rose—tilted, shuddering violently—then settled into balance as the tension evened out.

The survey boat was safe. The platform was safe. The crew was safe.

When it was finally secured, David let out a long breath he didn't even realise he'd been holding.

Bill folded his arms, watching the last of the dust drift into the air. "Well," he said, voice steady as ever, "that went sideways in a hurry."

David laughed—half relief, half disbelief. "You moved faster than my twenty-year-olds."

Bill shrugged. "Old habits. Hard to break." Then he turned to David with a faint smile. "Good calls out there. You kept your head."

Coming from a former Navy SEAL who had spent years managing life-and-death operations, the words carried more weight than any formal commendation.

From that day on, their professional respect deepened into something stronger. They had faced a dangerous moment together, made quick decisions under pressure, and saved lives because of it. And that forged a bond few men ever forget.

The harbour gradually transformed under their combined efforts—old concrete torn away, channels deepened, new berths taking shape like the ribs of a ship rising from the sand. And as the project advanced, David began to see that meeting Bill Meeks would become one of the most memorable professional relationships of his time in Kuwait.

Marbella

After the Mina Al Ahmadi project concluded, Bill surprised everyone—David included—by revealing his next venture. Instead of returning to engineering consultancy or diving operations, he had purchased a **nightclub in Marbella**, on Spain's glittering Costa del Sol. It was an unexpected move, but somehow entirely in character for a man who had already lived several lives in one.

Marbella in the late 1980s was a magnet for wealth, glamour, and international intrigue. It drew aristocrats, movie stars, oil magnates, and the occasional fugitive with a suspiciously quiet past. Bill's nightclub—stylish, discreet, and impeccably run—fit perfectly into this world. He had chosen the location well: tucked just off the Golden Mile, close enough to attract the high-profile crowd but private enough to assure them a sense of exclusivity.

Within months, the club became one of Marbella's most talked-about venues. Bill's reputation as a former U.S. Navy SEAL, combined with his sharp business sense and natural charm, created an aura that fascinated people. He operated the club with a precise balance of hospitality and security—no scandals, no reporters allowed no tolerance for troublemakers. Word spread quickly: if you wanted privacy, class, and company worth remembering, this was the place.

Soon, the guest list read like pages from an international who's who. **American senators**, holidaying far from the prying eyes of Washington, spent evenings in quiet conversation on the terrace. **European politicians**, escaping the stiff formality of their capitals, relaxed at Bill's bar with an ease they never enjoyed at home. Film stars drifted through, some seeking attention, others hoping to avoid it. Oil executives, old colleagues of Bill's from his commercial diving days, made his club their unofficial meeting spot whenever they passed through Spain.

Bill enjoyed the world he'd built there—not for the fame or the wealth, but for the constant sense of controlled unpredictability. Every night brought new faces, new stories, new secrets. Yet he remained the same steady presence he had been in Kuwait: calm, observant, respectful, and always two steps ahead of whatever might unfold.

David would later reflect that of all the careers Bill Meeks could have chosen after the disciplines of the Navy and the intensity of oilfield diving, running an elite nightclub in Marbella sounded like the least likely—and yet somehow the most perfectly suited to him. It was another adventure in a life full of them, and Bill embraced it with the same cool confidence he had once carried onboard military helicopters and offshore platforms.

In the months following the assassination attempt on Emir Sheikh Jaber, Kuwait entered a period of unease that rippled through every sector of the country—including the construction industry. Security tightened everywhere, checkpoints appeared along major roads, and government departments moved cautiously, sometimes paralysed by fear of further attacks. What had once been a fast-moving schedule of infrastructure and marine works suddenly slowed to a crawl.

For companies like David's, the shift was unmistakable. **Projects were postponed. Contracts that had looked certain evaporated overnight.**

Government ministries, once eager to push forward with harbour expansions, industrial dredging, and coastal developments, became hesitant. Budgets were frozen or quietly redirected into national defence and security measures. International consultants, alarmed by the instability, took their families home and declined new assignments.

Bit by bit, the workload dried up.

Where once David's company had been juggling multiple marine projects simultaneously, now the calendar was nearly empty—just a handful of small jobs and maintenance tasks, barely enough to justify the size of their workforce. The bustling office in Kuwait City grew quieter each week, phones ringing less, meetings cancelled or rescheduled indefinitely. Then came the layoffs.

They began subtly at first—short-term contracts not being renewed, junior staff encouraged to "take extended leave." But as the months dragged on and no new tenders appeared, the cuts became unavoidable. Skilled Dredgemasters, engineers, surveyors, welders—men who had spent years in the Gulf—found themselves without work, their final pay cheques accompanied by apologetic letters blaming "market conditions."

David saw the toll it took. Some men tried their luck in Saudi Arabia or the UAE, but even there, work was tightening. Others packed up their apartments and left Kuwait entirely, their departure evident in the growing number of empty flats, vacant parking spaces, and quiet evenings in previously lively expatriate neighbourhoods.

Even within David's own team, morale sank. There was an unspoken fear that anyone could be next. Every rumour of a cancelled contract spread like fire. Every closed-door meeting raised eyebrows. Men who had once been upbeat and chatty now kept their thoughts to themselves, their futures uncertain.

The sense of opportunity that had once defined Kuwait during the boom years of the 1970s and early 1980s had faded. In its place was a low, persistent anxiety—the feeling that the golden era had passed, and something darker was settling over the region.

For David, who had weathered many challenges in Kuwait, it was the first time he sensed that the stability he had built for Julie and Scott might not last forever.

And so, after a long discussion with Mr. Fadel, it was decided that David could be paid full indemnities and leave the company if he wanted to. If the situation would change, Mr. Fadel promised to re-employ David.

David decided he would now like to take a long holiday. Scott was now ready to continue his secondary education, and Scotland was now the plan.

Chapter 9-Return to Scotland

Before leaving Kuwait—knowing it might be for an indefinite period—Julie, David, and Scott began the difficult process of sorting through their belongings. They sold or gave away anything they couldn't ship back to the UK and spent several emotional days saying farewell to the friends who had become such a large part of their lives.

David received his full end-of-service benefits from the company, along with air tickets for the family to Inverness. With mixed feelings of relief and sadness, they boarded the plane and left the desert landscape behind.

When they arrived at the house in Inverness—the home they had purchased two years earlier but had barely lived in—they felt a renewed sense of anticipation. It was a chance to begin a new chapter, perhaps a more peaceful one.

Scott was enrolled at the local academy, and Julie threw herself into turning the house into a warm, welcoming home. Rooms that had stood mostly empty were now filled with the familiar sense of family life again. David, eager to make the place truly theirs, devoted his time to the garden. He even had a perimeter wall built along the front of the property, complete with wrought iron gates—a feature he had admired in other Highland homes.

For the first time in years, David did not rush immediately into finding work. After the constant pressure and long hours in Kuwait, he wanted something different—something that would allow him to be home every day and choose his own working hours. Eventually, after giving the matter careful thought, he applied to the Highland Regional Council for a taxi licence.

He wasn't granted a full taxicab licence, but he did receive a **Private Hire licence**, which had fewer privileges but suited him perfectly. He started small, advertising his new business locally and having a thousand business cards printed, which he handed out wherever he could.

The financial rewards were modest compared to what he had earned in Kuwait, but that no longer troubled him. He had saved well over the years, and for the first time, money wasn't the driving force. What mattered now was stability, family life, and the freedom to shape his days however he chose.

Scott's Adjustment

For Scott, settling into his new school in Inverness proved far more challenging than anyone had expected. Although he had been born in Scotland, he had spent almost his entire childhood abroad, and in many ways he felt more like a foreigner returning to a country he barely remembered.

From his very first day at the academy, he stood out—not deliberately, but unmistakably. His **English accent**, shaped by years in the Kuwait English School, drew attention immediately. Some of the local boys teased him for it; others simply regarded him with a kind of cautious curiosity. In a community where identity was tied closely to place, family, and heritage, Scott's lack of allegiance to anything distinctly Scottish made him seem, at first, like an outsider.

To make matters more complicated, Scott was academically **one year ahead** of the Scottish curriculum. His schooling in Kuwait had followed a British system that moved at a faster pace, particularly in maths and language skills. While this gave him confidence in the classroom, it also set him apart.

Teachers noticed his grasp of subjects, but his classmates—already wary of the boy with the "English-sounding voice"—sometimes interpreted his ability as showing off, even though that was never his intention.

The first few weeks were lonely. Scott missed the international community he had grown up in, where children came from every imaginable background and accents were a mixture of the world. In Kuwait, differences had been normal; in Inverness, they made him conspicuous.

But slowly, things began to change.

A few boys in his class, impressed by the stories Scott shared about life in Kuwait—desert heat, rooftop restaurants, swimming in the warm Arabian Gulf—started to include him in games at break time. They were fascinated by his tales of expat life, by the idea of living somewhere so far from their quiet Highland town. One boy in particular, a friendly lad named Callum, took to Scott early on. Callum wasn't bothered by accents or allegiances; he simply liked hearing about a world he had never seen.

Gradually, Scott found his footing. He joined in sports days, learned local slang, and even picked up enough knowledge about Scottish football to survive playground conversations. He still felt different at times—straddling two worlds, belonging fully to neither—but he was adapting, shaping a new identity from the mixture of all the places he had lived.

Julie often worried about him, but David reassured her: "Scott's tougher than he looks. He's been through more changes than most boys his age, and he's still smiling."

And indeed, in time, Scott made good friends and grew more confident. Although the transition had been rocky, he was learning not only how to fit in, but how to stand out in ways that mattered.

Scott Stands His Ground

Despite gradually finding his place at school, Scott still faced moments that tested him deeply. One boy in particular—bigger, rougher, and known for picking on anyone who seemed different—had singled him out. To this bully, Scott's English accent and quiet manner were an open invitation.

It began with name-calling and shoves in the corridor, but one afternoon it escalated. Scott came home pale and shaken, his left eye already swelling with a deep purple bruise. Above it, an ugly bump throbbed angrily beneath the skin.

Julie gasped when she saw him. "What on earth happened?"

Scott hesitated, eyes filling. "He... he head-butted me, Mum. For no reason."

David looked at his son carefully. He recognised the quiet humiliation, the way Scott avoided his gaze. It was a look he remembered from his own boyhood—a mixture of fear, anger, and shame.

Later, when they were alone, David sat beside him.

"Scott," he said gently, "you can't let this boy keep doing this to you."

"I'm scared, Dad," Scott whispered. "He's bigger than me. And he—he likes hurting people."

David placed a hand on his shoulder, firm but reassuring.

"He knows you're scared—that's why he keeps picking on you. But listen to me carefully: if you fight back, even if you lose, he'll think twice before ever laying a hand on you again."

Scott's lower lip trembled. "But what if he hurts me?"

"He already has," David said softly. "But next time you'll be ready. Tell him you want a fair fight. Stand your ground. You don't have to win—you just must show him you won't let him walk all over you."

It wasn't bravado; it was practicality. David had learned during his own rough childhood that bullies thrived on fear and faded the moment someone refused to bow to them.

The next day, Scott did exactly as his father had told him. Heart pounding, palms sweating, he approached the boy in the schoolyard and said, voice trembling, "If you want to fight, then do it properly. Just you and me. No surprises."

The bully stared at him, taken aback. This wasn't the reaction he expected from the "English boy." Word spread quickly, and soon a small circle formed. Scott braced himself, knowing his father was right—whether he won or lost mattered less than showing he wasn't afraid anymore.

The fight was short and scrappy. Scott took a few hits, but he landed one as well—enough to surprise the bully and knock him off his confidence. When it was over, both boys were bruised and panting, but Scott stayed on his feet.

From that day onward, the bullying stopped. The boy never bothered him again. And although Scott didn't feel proud of the fight itself, he carried a new sense of strength with him—a belief that he could stand up for himself when it mattered most.

When Scott came home after the fight, his shirt untucked and a smear of dirt on his cheek, Julie saw him standing in the doorway and felt her heart stop. Although he wasn't badly hurt, there was a tightness around his eyes—a mixture of exhaustion, pride, and the remnants of fear—that told her everything she needed to know.

"My God, Scott... what happened?" she asked, rushing toward him.

Scott hesitated for a moment, then quietly admitted, "Mum... I did what Dad told me. I—I stood up to him."

Julie froze. She had known there was a bullying problem but hearing that her son had confronted the boy, fists and all, filled her with a storm of emotions. Pride wrestled against fear, and fear wrestled against the instinctive wish to protect him from everything the world could throw at him.

"You fought him?" she whispered, her voice trembling.

Scott nodded, eyes downcast. "Just a fair fight. Like Dad said. And... he won't bother me again."

Julie pulled him into her arms. The hug lingered longer than usual. She felt the slight shaking in his shoulders—whether from adrenaline or relief, she couldn't be sure—and she realised how brave he had been. But the thought of her gentle, good-hearted boy having to defend himself physically made her chest ache.

That evening, after Scott went to his room, she confronted David in the kitchen.

"You told him to fight?" she said, keeping her voice low but unable to hide the upset in it.

David met her gaze calmly. "Julie, he had no choice. That boy wasn't going to stop. Scott had to show him he wasn't afraid."

Julie shook her head, torn between understanding and maternal instinct. "He's only a child."

"He's a child who stood up for himself today," David replied gently. "And look—he came home safe. And proud. That bully will leave him alone now."

Julie looked away, blinking back tears. "I just… I hate that it had to come to that."

David stepped closer, placing a reassuring hand on her arm. "So do I. But sometimes the world doesn't give us better options."

She sighed, letting the fear slowly melt into relief. Deep down, she knew David was right. Scott *had* needed to stand his ground—and he had done so with more courage than she had ever imagined.

Later that night, she checked on Scott as he slept. His face was peaceful, the hint of a bruise still visible beneath his eye. She brushed a hand lightly across his hair and whispered, almost to herself:

"My brave boy… I just want you safe."

And as she closed the door, she felt something shift—an acceptance that Scott, despite being her little boy, was growing into someone capable of facing the world on his own terms.

David, on hearing the outcome that evening, simply nodded and said, "That's my boy."

In the weeks that followed the fight, something subtle but unmistakable began to change in Scott. It wasn't that he became louder or boastful—far from it. Instead, a quiet steadiness settled over him, the kind of confidence that comes not from winning a battle, but from proving to oneself that fear doesn't have the final say.

He walked into school with more assurance than before. The cautious glances and whispered remarks from classmates slowly faded, replaced by nods of acknowledgment from boys who had watched him stand up to the bully. Even those who had previously kept their distance now seemed more willing to include him in games or group projects. Scott, who had once felt like an outsider with the "wrong accent" and no local ties, was now earning respect on his own terms.

Callum, the boy who had first befriended him, noticed the shift immediately. "You're different now," he told Scott one lunchtime. "Not scared anymore." Scott shrugged, but there was a small, knowing smile he couldn't quite hide.

Even in the classroom, his confidence showed. No longer worried that he'd be mocked for speaking up, Scott began raising his hand more often. His advanced schooling from Kuwait, once a point of awkwardness, now began working in his favour. Teachers praised his thoughtful answers and willingness to help others who struggled. Far from resenting him, many classmates now came to rely on him—especially in maths, where his Kuwaiti curriculum had placed him a full year ahead.

At home, Julie and David saw the difference too.

He was more relaxed in himself, quicker to laugh, more eager to try new things. He even began taking an interest in Scottish football—not because he felt pressured to fit in, but because he *wanted* to. The conversations at school no longer intimidated him; he felt able to join in, to contribute. For the first time since their return from Kuwait, he felt he belonged.

One evening, after Scott had gone to bed, David said quietly to Julie, "He's coming into his own."

Julie smiled, though a little wistfully. "Yes... he is. Our boy's growing up."

And he was. The boy who had once come home bruised and shaken was now learning to navigate this new world with resilience and self-belief. It wasn't the fight that had changed him—it was the courage he had found within himself because of it.

After they had been back home in Inverness for a few weeks, Julie began looking for something meaningful to fill her days. She soon found a place at a local charity shop, working as a volunteer. The shop sold donated clothing, books, and all sorts of second-hand household items—each sale contributing to a cause close to her heart.

The proceeds were used to fund respite care for people in the community who were looking after children with disabilities or family members who required constant support. Julie found the work deeply satisfying. Not only did it give her a daily routine and new friends within the community, but she also felt she was doing something genuinely helpful—something that made a difference in the lives of people who carried heavy burdens.

It wasn't glamorous work, but Julie approached it with quiet dedication, grateful for the sense of purpose and belonging it brought into this new phase of her life.

Julie quickly discovered that the charity shop was more than just a workplace—it was a little community of its own. The volunteers came from all walks of life: retired teachers, widows looking for companionship, young mothers wanting a few hours away from home, and a handful of students eager to gain experience.

What struck Julie most was how welcoming they were. On her first day, the older ladies—often the early-morning crew—made her a cup of tea, sat her down in the tiny staff kitchen, and asked about her time in Kuwait. Before long, she found herself sharing stories she hadn't expected to talk about: the desert heat, the souks, the call to prayer echoing before dawn. They listened with fascination, amazed by her experiences and the life she had lived abroad.

Over time, Julie built close friendships. She learned who loved gardening, who baked cakes on Thursdays, who was always ready with a joke when the day felt long. They laughed together while sorting through bags of donated clothes—sometimes marvelling at the quality, sometimes shaking their heads at the oddities people chose to give away.

These small, ordinary moments became the foundation of something she had been missing: a sense of belonging. Working at the charity shop gave Julie more than a routine; it restored her confidence in ways she hadn't anticipated. After years of following David's career around the world—adapting to Kuwait, navigating expatriate life, uprooting again for Scotland—she had lost a sense of her own independence.

But here, in Inverness, she found a place where her contributions mattered.

She became known for her warm manner with customers, her eye for arranging displays, and her ability to listen without judgement when someone needed to talk. People gravitated toward her gentleness. The manager often said, "Julie, the shop feels calmer when you're here."

As her confidence grew, so did her social circle. She began receiving invitations to coffee mornings, charity events, and even the occasional dinner at a volunteer's home. Outside the shop, she'd bump into familiar faces at the supermarket or on the high street, and they'd stop to chat as if she'd lived there all her life.

The isolation she had felt during those early weeks in Scotland began to fade. Julie was becoming part of the community—not just as David's wife or Scott's mother, but as **her own person**, valued and appreciated.

And in quiet moments, folding clothes behind the counter or chatting with customers, she realised something important: she no longer felt like a stranger returning from a distant life. She felt grounded. She felt at home.

Please provide a few paragraphs about the private hire experience of David leading to how he knew this would not satisfy him as a career and began making moves to look for work in his chosen profession - dredging and marine construction

Private Hire Experience

David settled into his role as a Private Hire driver with a mixture of curiosity and practicality. At first, he found it enjoyable in its own modest way. There was a certain freedom in choosing his own hours, deciding which bookings to accept, and being home with Julie and Scott every night—something he hadn't experienced for years.

His customers were a varied mix. Some were elderly residents needing lifts to medical appointments; others were tourists exploring the Highlands, delighted to have a driver who knew the area well. He enjoyed the conversations, the small insights into people's lives, and the simple satisfaction of providing a helpful service.

But as the months rolled on, the novelty began to fade.

David found himself working long stretches of the day for only modest returns. The Highland weather could be harsh, and he would often sit in the car waiting for the next call, engine idling to keep warm while rain hammered the windscreen. Some days were busy, others painfully quiet. And although he was grateful for the independence the job allowed him, he felt something important was missing.

Driving people from one place to another didn't challenge him—not in the way he was used to. There were no crews to manage, no technical problems to solve, no large-scale operations demanding his judgement and experience. He missed the sense of purpose that had always come with dredging and marine construction—the planning, the problem-solving, the pressure, and the satisfaction of seeing a project take shape under his guidance.

Julie noticed the restlessness slowly creeping in.

"You're bored," she said one evening as David sat at the kitchen table, staring at his booking diary with little enthusiasm.

He didn't deny it. "It's fine... but it's not *me*. Not really."

David knew it too. The work paid the bills, but it didn't engage his mind. He had spent years overseeing complex marine operations in Kuwait—projects involving vast machinery, coordination of multinational crews, and negotiations with government officials. Compared to that, private hire driving felt like walking when he had once been flying.

Eventually, the decision became clear. He needed to return to the industry he knew best—the work that had defined most of his adult life. The dredging world was specialised, but David had decades of experience and a reputation that carried weight. He began making discreet enquiries, reaching out to old contacts, former colleagues, even competitors who might have heard of openings in the UK or abroad.

He dusted off his CV, updated it with his Kuwaiti projects, and wrote letters to several marine contracting firms. He read trade journals again, checking which companies had secured new harbour developments or port expansions. A spark returned to him—the same spark he'd felt in Kuwait when a new project was on the horizon.

And although he kept driving for the time being, he knew it was only temporary. His future, as far as he could see, still lay in the world of dredgers, breakwaters, and marine construction.

That was where he belonged. And he was ready to start the next chapter.

The Family's Reaction

When David finally shared with Julie and Scott that he was thinking of returning to marine construction, the reaction was layered relief, worry, acceptance, and a familiar sense of inevitability.

Julie listened quietly as he explained how unfulfilled he felt driving the private hire car, how he missed the challenges and responsibility of his old profession, and how he had started sending out feelers to companies across the UK.

She wasn't surprised. Not really.

Julie had seen the restlessness building in him for months—the way he lingered over marine engineering magazines, the spark in his eyes when discussing old projects, the sighs he thought she didn't hear when he realised another day had passed with nothing more taxing than airport runs and shopping trips. She knew the work he did in Kuwait had been intense, sometimes dangerous, often exhausting—but it had also given him purpose.

"It's who you are, David," she finally said, placing a hand over his. "I don't want you to stay in a job that makes you unhappy. But…" She paused, her voice softening. "I just want you safe."

That was her fear—the return to long hours, to distant travel, to the uncertainties of an industry tied to tides and storms and unpredictable waters. She had enjoyed having him home every day. So had Scott.

Scott's reaction was quieter but honest. Sitting at the table, he chewed the inside of his cheek before speaking.

"Does this mean you'll be away again?" he asked.

David hesitated. "Yes. Hopefully not for lengthy periods, but some projects need time on-site."

Scott looked down at his hands. "I like having you around, Dad."

The words pierced David more deeply than any criticism could have. He reached over and squeezed Scott's shoulder.

"I know, son. And I promise… if I do go back to dredging, I'll make sure it's different this time. More time at home. I'll choose carefully."

Julie nodded at that, grateful for the reassurance, though still anxious. "Whatever happens," she said, "we'll face it together. We always have."

The conversation didn't end with perfect clarity or immediate decisions, but what mattered was this: they understood each other. They recognised David's need for purpose, just as he recognised their need for security and stability.

And beneath the tension, there was something else—a quiet strength that had carried them through every chapter of their lives so far. Whatever came next, they would manage it as a family.

A Job Offer

It happened on a grey, drizzly Inverness morning—a morning that looked much like any other. David was sorting through his private hire paperwork when the phone rang. He almost didn't answer it; the number was unfamiliar, likely another client asking for a late-night airport run.

"Hello, David Bentley speaking."

The voice on the other end had a crisp, professional tone—British, but with the clipped inflection of someone used to international work. It was the operations director of a marine contracting company based in Aberdeen. They had received David's CV, reviewed his experience in Kuwait and the Gulf, and wanted to discuss a senior position on a new coastal development project.

As the conversation unfolded, David felt a rush of adrenaline he hadn't experienced since his days overseas. The questions came quickly—project management experience, dredging methodology, personnel leadership—and he answered each one with clarity and confidence. By the end of the call, the operations director spoke the words David had been hoping for:

"We'd like to offer you the position, David—pending a final meeting. The job requires some travel, but the site work is rotational. Plenty of time at home."

David thanked him, trying to keep his voice steady. When he hung up, the house around him felt unusually still, as if the air itself was waiting for his next move.

Julie was in the kitchen when David came through, the excitement in his expression unmistakable. She listened quietly as he recounted the call, her eyes widening with each detail.

A job. A real position. A return to his profession.

Part of her felt relieved—grateful that David had found something meaningful after months of restlessness. She wanted him to be fulfilled, to feel useful, to reclaim the identity that private hire driving could never offer. But as the reality settled in, a familiar anxiety tugged at her.

She remembered the long days waiting in Kuwait, the worry when he was offshore or supervising high-pressure projects. She remembered how much they had leaned on each other during difficult times. And she feared—not unreasonably—that marine construction might once again pull him away.

"You're happy," she said softly, searching his face.

"I am," David admitted. "But I won't take it unless you're comfortable with it."

Julie looked down at the tea towel in her hands, twisting it unconsciously. She wanted to be brave. She wanted to support him. And she also wanted her husband home.

"I just… I need time to let it sink in," she finally said. "I know it's right for you, David. And I'll stand by you. I always have. But I'd be lying if I said I'm not scared of losing the life we've built here."

David wrapped his arms around her, reassuring her without words.

When Scott came home from school, David sat him down and explained the offer. Scott listened in silence, absorbing each detail.

"So, you'll be away?" he asked quietly.

"Sometimes," David replied. "Not like before. Not for months. Just short rotations. I'll be home more than I'm gone."

Scott nodded, trying to appear grown-up about it, though the flicker of worry in his eyes betrayed him. He had grown used to having his father nearby helping with homework, playing football in the garden, being part of everyday life.

"Will you still be here for weekends?" he asked.

"Most of them," David assured him.

Scott hesitated, then said, "If it makes you happy, Dad… then it's okay. I just don't want it to be like Kuwait again."

David pulled him close. "It won't be. I promise."

Scott believed him—he wanted to believe him—and though the adjustment would take time, he carried himself with the same resilience he had shown since settling into his new school. He understood that adults sometimes had to make hard choices, and he trusted his father enough to know that the family would face whatever came next together.

David's Interview

David travelled to Aberdeen a week later for the interview. He arrived early, dressed neatly, with a folder of reference letters under his arm—though he suspected his years of experience would speak louder than anything on paper. The meeting took place in a modern glass-fronted office overlooking the harbour. The operations director, along with a senior engineer and HR representative, welcomed him with firm handshakes and an air of genuine interest.

The interview flowed naturally. They asked about his offshore platform restoration in Kuwait, his dredging operations under pressure, his ability to manage multinational crews, and his leadership style. David answered with calm confidence, drawing on decades of knowledge. As the questions continued, he could sense their enthusiasm growing.

By the end of the meeting, the operations director pushed the contract across the table.

"We'd be very pleased to have you on board, David," he said. "Your experience is exactly what we need."

David reviewed the terms—fair salary, rotational schedule, and reasonable expectations. He thought of Julie, of Scott, of the life they had begun rebuilding. This job offered the balance he needed: meaningful work without uprooting the family again.

"I accept," he said, signing the contract with a steady hand.

Contract Completed

Over the next thirteen months, David committed himself fully to the coastal development project. He handled everything from dredging operations to breakwater construction, navigating tides, storms, and demanding deadlines. The company respected him; younger engineers sought his advice; senior managers relied on his judgement. It was hard work, but it felt right—like returning to an identity that had been waiting for him.

When the final phase wrapped up and the last reports were submitted, David stood on the breakwater and watched the waves crash against the newly built armour rock. It was a good project; one he was proud of. For the first time in years, he felt both accomplished and at peace.

He was back home, thinking about taking some well-earned rest, when the phone rang.

A Call from Kuwait

The call came in the early afternoon. David instantly recognised the voice on the other end, warm and formal all at once.

"Mr. David... this is Fadel Abu Abbas."

David straightened in his chair. It had been years since they'd spoken, but the tone—respectful, decisive—was unmistakable.

"Fadel! It's good to hear from you. How are things in Kuwait?"

"We are preparing for a very large marine project," Fadel replied. "A major expansion... one of the biggest in our company's history. We need someone with your experience. Someone we trust."

David felt his pulse quicken.

Fadel continued, "Your performance with us was exceptional, David. I would be very pleased—personally pleased—if you would consider returning. I am prepared to offer terms that I believe you will find... very agreeable."

The phrasing was deliberate. The meaning unmistakable.

It was an offer that suggested a high salary, senior responsibility, and the kind of respect David had worked a lifetime to earn. The sort of offer that rarely came twice.

For a long moment, David said nothing, absorbing the weight of it. He thought of Julie, Scott, their settled life in Inverness, and how far they had come since leaving the desert behind. He also thought of Kuwait—the challenges, the heat, the camaraderie, the sense of purpose that came with running major marine operations. "David," Fadel said gently, "I would not call you if it were not important. This project needs the best. And you are one of the best men I have ever worked with." It was, indeed, an offer very hard to refuse.

That evening, after dinner, David gathered Julie and Scott in the living room. They could tell something was on his mind—the kind of quiet intensity David always carried when weighing a serious decision.

"I had a call today," he began, folding his hands thoughtfully. "From Kuwait."

Julie's eyes widened immediately. Scott looked up from the carpet, alert.

"It was Fadel," David continued. "He wants me back. The company has a major new project starting soon. A big one. He's offering me a senior role."

There was a long moment of silence.

Scott was the first to speak, his voice steady but uncertain. "Would we have to move back to Kuwait?"

David shook his head. "No. The arrangement would be rotational. I'd work in Kuwait for a period, then come home for several weeks. You two would stay here."

Julie sat back slowly, absorbing the words. "And... what exactly are they offering you?"

David took a breath. "Quite a lot, actually."

Fadel's Offer

He listed the details carefully, conscious of the weight each one carried:

- **A senior management position**—effectively second-in-command of the entire marine works division.

- **A salary far higher** than anything available in the UK: a tax-free package that could secure their financial future.

- **Full expatriate benefits**, including private medical insurance and generous allowances.

- **Accommodation provided** in Kuwait—a fully furnished villa or high-end apartment, available for his use during work rotations.

- **Annual flights home**, in addition to rotation leave flights.

- **A long-term contract**, with substantial performance bonuses tied to project milestones.

- **Authority to build and manage his own team**—something David excelled at.

"It's the sort of offer that doesn't come often," David said quietly. "And Fadel made it clear he wants *me* for this. He said it personally."

Julie nodded slowly, her expression deeply conflicted.

The room grew still, filled with a mixture of possibility and worry.

Julie spoke first, her voice soft but weighted.

"I knew this might happen someday. I knew someone would try to pull you back into the big projects. And I want you to be happy, David—truly, I do." She paused, looking down at her hands.

"But Kuwait... it was such a huge part of our lives. Going back, even part-time... it scares me a little."

David moved closer, taking her hand. "It scares me too," he admitted. "I don't want to uproot us again. I don't want to lose the home we've built here."

Scott listened, biting his lip. The idea of his father being away—even part-time—unnerved him. "How long would you be gone at a time?" he asked.

"Six weeks on, one week off," David said. "Sometimes less. It depends on the stage of the project."

Scott nodded but looked uncertain. "I just... I like you being here, Dad."

David pulled him into a gentle embrace. "I know, son. And I love being here. But I must consider our future too."

Julie looked at David, her eyes softening. "You've always done what's best for us. Always. If this is something you feel you need to do... I'll support you. I just need time to come to terms with it."

David nodded, grateful yet torn. The offer shimmered before him—opportunity, challenge, respect, security. But the cost... the cost was time away from the two people who mattered most.

For the first time in years, he felt pulled in two directions—with no easy answer.

Leaving Scotland — March 1989

March arrived sooner than any of them expected. The Highlands were still cold, the mornings edged with frost, and the air carried that crisp scent of early spring. David packed his suitcase slowly, folding shirts beside work boots, placing documents carefully into a leather folder he hadn't used since Kuwait.

On the morning of his departure, the three of them drove to the airport in a quiet, reflective mood. Scott sat in the back seat, clutching a book he planned to give David for the long flight. Julie held David's hand the entire journey.

At the terminal, the emotions finally found their way to the surface. Julie's eyes glistened as David hugged her tightly.

"You come home to us safe," she whispered.

"I will," he promised. "And this time, it will be different. I'll be home more than I'm away."

He knelt to face Scott. "Look after your mum. And study hard. I'll be back before you know it."

Scott threw his arms around him. "I will, Dad... I promise."

When the final call for boarding echoed through the airport, David picked up his bag and took one last look at his family. Julie stood tall, chin trembling slightly but her eyes full of love. Scott waved, trying to smile bravely.

David stepped through the gate, feeling both the weight of leaving and the pull of purpose ahead.

As the plane lifted from the runway and the Scottish landscape faded beneath the clouds, he knew he was crossing into another chapter—one filled with challenges, opportunities, and the familiar heat and hum of the Gulf.

Kuwait was calling him back. And this time, he was returning on his own terms.

Chapter 10 -Batchelor Status

The Prestigious Amiri Diwan Project

When David returned to Kuwait, he quickly realised that this was not just another contract—this was a project of national pride, political importance, and architectural ambition. Fadel had not exaggerated its scale or significance.

David had been brought back to help oversee key marine and coastal works on the **Amiri Diwan Project**, a massive undertaking valued at **over three hundred million dollars**. It was one of the largest and most symbolic construction initiatives Kuwait had embarked upon since the early days of oil prosperity.

The project comprised several monumental components:

1. Al Diwan Al Amiri Building

This was to be the heart of Kuwait's leadership—an ornate and imposing structure designed to serve as the official residence and ceremonial headquarters of the Emir. The building's design blended traditional Islamic architecture with modern engineering, combining elegant domes, expansive courtyards, and marble interiors with advanced structural systems.

2. The Crown Prince's Building

Equally impressive was the Crown Prince's building, a companion complex tailored for administrative and governmental functions. Its significance was not merely architectural, but symbolic: it represented continuity and stability within Kuwait's ruling structure.

3. The Cabinet Meeting Hall and Secretariat

A major part of the project was a purpose-built hall for the Cabinet and its General Secretariat—a place where high-level governmental decisions would be made. The hall was designed with cutting-edge acoustic engineering, elaborate security features, and a sweeping interior layout meant to convey authority and unity.

4. A Uniquely Designed Lagoon

Perhaps the most striking element—and the one directly tied to David's expertise—was the **artificial lagoon**: a stunning water feature enclosed by a robust **outer breakwater**. The lagoon was planned as a tranquil, ceremonial space, offering spectacular reflections of the Diwan buildings and serving as a protective barrier from coastal conditions.

The marine works were extensive and complex:

- **Dredging the lagoon basin** to precise depths using the dredged materials to reclaim land.

- **Constructing the outer breakwater** with armour rock and reinforced foundation layers

- **Expanding and stabilising the shoreline** to support the surrounding structures

- **Coordinating marine traffic and safety zones** during construction

- **Ensuring environmental compliance** in a sensitive coastal area

This was not just a technical challenge—it was a matter of national prestige. Every stage required accuracy, discipline, and a level of quality that allowed no margin for error.

David's Role

Fadel appointed David as **Senior Marine Works Manager**, giving him direct authority over dredging operations, land reclamation, breakwater construction, marine logistics, and interface coordination with architectural and civil engineering teams. The responsibility was immense, but so was the trust Fadel placed in him.

"Mr. David," Fadel said during their first meeting, "this project will define Kuwait for generations. I need someone who can think clearly, act decisively, and lead with integrity. I know you are that man."

David felt the weight of those words—but also the honour. After years of uncertainty and restlessness, he was once again at the helm of a project that demanded the very best of him.

Challenges

From the moment David stepped onto the project site, he realised this job was going to test every skill he had acquired over decades in the industry. The Amiri

Diwan Project was enormous, and the marine works functioned as the foundation upon which all the land-based construction depended. Any delay offshore would ripple through the entire programme, affecting structural, architectural, mechanical, and ceremonial deadlines.

The team itself was a complex mosaic of nationalities:

- Dutch dredging specialists

- Filipino and Indian marine labour crews

- Egyptian and Syrian civil engineers

- US & British consultants

- Kuwaiti government inspectors

- Pakistani welders

- Italian marble suppliers for the buildings

Each group brought its own expertise, its own rhythm, its own way of communicating. But they also brought cultural differences, conflicting expectations, and deeply ingrained working habits that did not always blend smoothly.

David often found himself mediating disputes over equipment allocation, interpreting technical misunderstandings, or smoothing over tensions caused by cultural misinterpretations. The breakwater teams needed the dredgers to move faster, the dredgers blamed survey delays, and the surveyors blamed sudden specification changes from the architects.

And through it all, the clock was ticking—loudly.

The Emir's office expected progress reports weekly. Government ministers toured the site regularly, flanked by security personnel and aides carrying clipboards. If a milestone slipped, everyone knew it would reach the highest political levels within hours.

David's days were long, starting before sunrise and ending well after dark. His phone never stopped ringing. His radio never fell silent. Yet he held the chaos together with a steady hand—calm, methodical, and seasoned by years of managing high-pressure marine works in harsh conditions.

Still, even he sometimes felt the strain.

Political Sensitivity and Pressure

What made the Amiri Diwan Project particularly challenging was its political importance. It wasn't simply a government job—it was a national symbol. The Diwan, the Crown Prince's building, the Cabinet Meeting Hall… these were institutions at the heart of Kuwait's identity and governance.

Failure was not an option. Not even minor embarrassment.

Every delay risked scrutiny. Every misstep risked diplomatic tension. Every safety issue risked headlines—and in a region where image and prestige carry immense weight, that was unacceptable.

On several occasions, David was summoned to high-level meetings to explain why tides had hindered dredging progress, why a shipment of armour rock had arrived late, or why survey results required rework. He found himself addressing not only engineers but ministers, advisors, and sometimes even members of the ruling family.

The stakes were high:

- **Security protocols tightened** after regional political incidents.

- **Media attention grew** as rumours circulated about the project's scale.

- **Questions in parliament** occasionally referenced the timeline.

- **Diplomatic visitors** toured the site, raising the project's visibility even further.

The pressure was relentless.

David knew that, more than any technical challenge, the politics surrounding the Amiri Diwan Project would test him the hardest. It required diplomacy, patience, and a calm resolve that not many in the field possessed.

Yet Fadel trusted him completely—and that trust mattered. It gave David the confidence to navigate the complex environment, to pull disparate teams together, and to push progress forward despite the obstacles.

The result was a marine works operation that, despite constant scrutiny and logistical challenges, began to move steadily in the right direction.

Julie and Scott Adjust to David's New Schedule

Life in Inverness settled into a new rhythm after David returned to Kuwait. It wasn't easy—at least not at first. The house felt quieter, the evenings longer, and simple routines like dinner or watching a television programme carried a faint sense of absence. Julie often found herself listening for the sound of David's car on the driveway, then remembering he was thousands of miles away under the desert sun.

Yet the rotational nature of his new contract softened the separation. Instead of being gone for months at a time, David was away only for several weeks before returning home for an extended break. This made all the difference. There was always a date circled on the calendar—**a reunion to look forward to**.

Scott, now older and more emotionally resilient, dealt with the schedule in his own quiet way. He threw himself into schoolwork, football practice, and weekends with friends. Though he missed David, the predictable cycle of departures and returns gave him stability. He counted down the days until his father's homecoming with excitement rather than anxiety.

Sometimes he even wrote David letters—full of school gossip, football scores, and little doodles of dredgers and breakwaters—letters that David kept in the drawer beside his bed in Kuwait.

Julie's Adjustment

Julie had already adapted once—from Kuwait's warmth to Scotland's cold, from a bustling expat social life to volunteering in a Highland charity shop. Now she faced a different kind of adjustment: keeping the home running smoothly while David worked halfway across the world.

But she handled it with quiet determination.

She continued volunteering at the charity shop, deepening friendships with the other ladies. She managed the household finances, maintained the garden when David was away, and made sure Scott stayed focused on school. Their Inverness house became her sanctuary—a place she could shape, improve, and fill with warmth in David's absence.

Of course, there were moments of loneliness. Nights when the wind howled across the canal and the house felt too big, too silent.

But Julie had grown stronger through the years, and she knew this sacrifice was temporary—and necessary.

More importantly, she knew David came home to her with pride and gratitude, never taking her strength for granted.

Leave Periods:

When David returned from Kuwait, the entire house seemed to come alive.

Scott would race down the stairs at the sound of the door opening, and Julie—tears threatening but smiling—would wrap her arms around David as though anchoring him back to the soil of Scotland itself.

They treated each leave period as **precious time**, never to be wasted.

- **Family drives** along Loch Ness or over the bridge to the Black Isle

- **Walks together** along the River Ness, talking about everything and nothing

- **Quiet evenings** with Julie and David curled up on the sofa, enjoying a normality they once feared they'd never have

- **Meals out**, celebrating small victories and cherishing the simple privilege of being together

- **Scott showing his father school projects**, football trophies, or new skills learned while David was away

David felt the contrast sharply—one month he was standing on a breakwater under the searing Gulf sun, coordinating multinational crews under political pressure; the next he was helping Scott with homework, fixing a loose garden gate, or laughing with Julie over their favourite comedy show.

The balance felt right. Hard-earned. Deeply appreciated.

For Julie and Scott, the knowledge that David *always returned*—that his work abroad was temporary and controlled—made the absences bearable. And for David, those reunions made every demanding day in Kuwait worth enduring.

They were no longer a family uprooted by circumstance. They were a family strengthened by choice, sacrifice, and the rhythm of coming together again and again.

The Political Climate

When David returned to Kuwait in 1989, he quickly sensed that the country was no longer the same as the one he had left years earlier. Beneath the familiar bustle of construction sites, crowded souks, and the shimmer of the Gulf, there was a new undercurrent—a quiet tension woven into everyday life.

Throughout the late 1980s, regional instability had begun to reshape Kuwait's political atmosphere. The country still carried the scars of the Iran–Iraq War, in which it had openly supported Iraq. Though the war had ended in 1988, its aftershocks continued to reverberate. There were whispers of extremist groups still harbouring resentment, and political analysts speculated that Kuwait's strategic alliances had earned it new enemies as well as old ones.

Government buildings, embassies, and major infrastructure projects—including the very one David was now helping to build—operated under heightened security protocols. Armed checkpoints became more common. Police presence increased. Visitors to official sites were screened more thoroughly. For the first time in years, Kuwait felt uncertain of what might come next.

Economic Shifts and Social Nervousness

The Kuwaiti economy, though buoyed by its vast oil revenues, had begun showing early signs of strain. Oil prices fluctuated sharply, and some government spending slowed. Certain expatriate communities, sensing instability, started planning exits or positioning themselves for quick moves should political tensions escalate.

David noticed the subtle behavioural changes:

- Senior officials were more guarded in conversations.

- Project meetings often included security briefings.

- Rumours travelled fast across worksites—of border tensions, military movements, diplomatic disagreements.

And while most of the population carried on with daily life, many Kuwaitis and expatriates alike felt an unspoken anxiety, a sense that the region's fragile equilibrium might soon tilt.

Growing Diplomatic Tensions

Meanwhile, relations between Kuwait and its neighbour Iraq were becoming increasingly strained. Publicly, the two nations spoke of cooperation and reconstruction after the Iran–Iraq War. Privately, Iraq—burdened by immense war debts—began accusing Kuwait of unfair oil production practices and economic sabotage.

David, though not involved in politics, could not avoid hearing the conversations that floated through cafés, offices, and even staff canteens:

- Iraq protested Kuwait's oil output.

- Kuwait refused to write off Iraq's debts.

- Border disputes resurfaced.

- Regional newspapers printed increasingly sharp commentary.

These tensions had not yet escalated into open conflict, but they were no longer ignorable. Even Fadel, normally calm and measured, occasionally hinted that the ministry wanted projects completed *quickly*, before any further instability could threaten progress.

A Country Holding Its Breath

By mid-1989 and early 1990, Kuwait felt like a place holding its breath. Life continued—shopping malls stayed busy, families picnicked along the Corniche, and construction cranes still dotted the skyline—but beneath the surface, the atmosphere had changed.

David, moving between the quiet stability of his home life in Scotland and the tightening political climate of Kuwait, could feel the contrast distinctly. Each time he flew back into Kuwait International Airport, he sensed the tension a little more clearly in the air, in the tone of conversations, in the worried glances exchanged by long-term expatriates.

No one could predict what would happen next. But many had begun to suspect that something was coming. And they were right.

Chapter 10 - War

It was **Wednesday, 1st August 1990**, and David was, as usual, having his evening meal in the restaurant at the Sultan Centre in Salmiya. The place had become something of a haven for him during his rotations—bright, air-conditioned, and always filled with a mix of locals and expatriates going about their evening routines.

Because he frequented the restaurant so often, David had come to know several of the regular customers. One of them was a young Kuwaiti named **Ahmed**, a pleasant fellow in his early twenties who served in the Kuwait Army. They had struck up a casual friendship over shared meals and small conversations about work, football, and life in Kuwait.

That evening, Ahmed spotted David and walked straight toward his table, his expression more serious than usual.
"May I join you?" he asked quietly.
"Of course," David said, gesturing to the empty seat. "Good to see you, Ahmed."

They exchanged a few pleasantries, but David could sense that something was weighing on the young man's mind. Ahmed glanced around the room, lowered his voice, and leaned in.

"David... there is something you should know," he said. "At the northern border... Iraqi troops. Thousands of them. Tanks, armour, everything. They've been gathering for two days now."

David paused, fork halfway to his mouth. "Troops? At the border? For what reason?"
Ahmed shook his head. "No one knows. Our officers are worried. Some say it is only an exercise, a show of force... but others believe it could be more." He hesitated, then added, "Much more."

A chill ran through David despite the cool restaurant air. He had sensed growing tension for months, but hearing this from a soldier—a young man who looked genuinely troubled—made it feel suddenly real, suddenly urgent.

Ahmed leaned back, eyes narrowing thoughtfully. "Be careful, my friend. Things may be about to change."

The clatter of dishes and the murmur of diners continued around them, but for David, the atmosphere had shifted. Something ominous was unfolding, and although he didn't yet know it, the next twenty-four hours would alter Kuwait—and his life—forever.

When David stepped out of the Sultan Centre that night, the heavy humidity of the Kuwaiti summer wrapped around him like a damp blanket. But it wasn't the heat that troubled him—it was Ahmed's warning. The young soldier's tone, the urgency in his eyes, lingered in David's mind with an unsettling weight.

He walked to his car slowly, scanning the quiet street. Nothing seemed out of place—families still shopping, neon lights flickering, traffic humming along the Gulf Road. Yet David felt the uneasy sense that beneath the normality, something was shifting.

As he drove back to his apartment in Salmiya, news reports on the radio were subdued, avoiding speculation. Only a brief mention hinted at "regional tensions" and "heightened military activity near the border." David switched it off. He preferred silence to half-truths.

In his apartment, he tried to read, then to watch television, but his mind kept drifting back to Ahmed's words: *Thousands of troops... tanks... something more.* By midnight, he had given up trying to sleep.

Around 2:00 a.m., David stood at his window, looking out over the dimly lit streets of Dasman. Kuwait City, normally glowing even at night, looked unusually subdued. There was a stillness—a strange heaviness in the air—as though the city itself sensed danger approaching.

Just after 3:00 a.m., he heard distant rumbling. At first, he thought it was thunder, though the skies were clear. A moment later, a deeper sound followed—low, rhythmic, mechanical. Tanks.
The Gulf War would later be recorded in history books as beginning at dawn on **2nd August 1990**, but the truth was that Kuwait felt the invasion before the sun rose. Iraqi forces were already on the move.

David's heart thudded as he closed the curtains. He checked the locks on his door, then sat on the edge of his bed, listening.
3:30 a.m. Again—distant thuds, the unmistakable echo of armoured vehicles.
4:00 a.m. The sky began to lighten, a faint grey glow stretching over the Gulf. Then it happened.

At **4:30 a.m.**, explosions rippled through the city. David jolted upright as the building shook slightly. The unmistakable sound of anti-aircraft fire cracked across the sky, followed by the roar of jet engines streaking low over the rooftops.

He rushed to the balcony, opened the door cautiously, and peered out. Dark smoke plumes were rising in the direction of Kuwait City. Sirens wailed. Cars screeched along the streets as panicked civilians tried to flee or reach relatives. David's phone began ringing—friends, colleagues, expatriates all calling with the same frantic question: "Have you heard what's happening?"
Yes. He had heard. And he knew, without doubt now, that Kuwait had been invaded. Or was it coup état?

He dialled home immediately. Nothing. The international lines were overloaded. He tried again. Busy. A third time. No connection.

At one point, David looked out from his apartment window and noticed a Kuwait Transport Company (KTC) bus parked across the main road below. His first thought was that a VIP might be visiting the Emir, and that the police had blocked the road using the bus to manage traffic. He was wrong.

While watching from the window, he heard the strange noise he'd noticed earlier only this time, it was louder and unmistakable. **Gunfire.**
Then, across the parking lot opposite the building, he saw a soldier sprinting, a radio pack strapped to his back with a long antenna bouncing behind him. This was the parking area adjacent to the **Kuwait State Security Building**, directly across from where he lived.
David's immediate thought was: *"It's a coup d'état. The Kuwaiti Army must be trying to seize the palace and capture the Emir."* He was wrong again.

David grabbed his briefcase and took the elevator down to the lobby.
One of the Filipina housemaids was at the reception desk. She saw him heading for the door and shouted, **"Sir, don't go outside! Danger!"**

True to his usual nature, David thanked her—and walked straight out anyway toward his car, parked about twenty metres from the entrance.
But as he descended the front steps, he was hit by the deafening, unmistakable sound of **heavy machine-gun fire**, very close by.

Instinct took over. He spun on his heels and sprinted back inside the building as fast as he could move.
Throwing himself behind the reception counter, he found two housemaids and another guest already crouched there, trembling. This was his wake-up call:
Do not leave the building.

Across the street, the State Security Building was under direct assault. It was clearly a primary target for the invading forces.

By around 6:00 a.m., several residents—shaken awake by explosions and gunfire—gathered in the building's ground-floor common areas, talking anxiously, trying to understand what was happening.

Around this time, David succeeded in getting a phone line through to the UK. He woke **Julie** and told her there was trouble in Kuwait. She was distraught, but David reassured her as best he could.

Shortly afterwards, he approached a man he hadn't seen before—a fellow with a distinctive **Saddam-style moustache**—and asked his opinion about what was unfolding. David was still unsure whether this was internal or external conflict. "Are those Kuwaiti soldiers out there?" David asked.
The man laughed—coldly.
"These Kuwaitis are like girls," he scoffed. "Our guards will eat them. Kuwait is ours now."
With that, he walked straight out of the building toward an armoured vehicle parked nearby. The soldiers greeted him with immediate respect. David realised he must have been a ranking officer in the Iraqi Army, dressed in civilian clothes. He never saw him again.

A Sky Filled with Helicopters
Around **10:00 a.m.**, the sound of helicopters drew David to the roof. What he saw stunned him.
The sky—stretching as far as he could see—was filled with **helicopters**. Hundreds of them. Gunships, troop carriers, smaller aircraft—in every direction, at various altitudes.
It was like watching a war movie, except this was real—too real.

The sight made the hair on the back of his neck stand on end. He would later describe it as one of the most surreal and terrifying visions of his life. After about 45 minutes, many of the helicopters disappeared—presumably landing throughout Kuwait to deploy soldiers—though dozens still circled above.

By **11:30 a.m.**, curiosity and concern compelled David to try venturing out. He went outside, started his car, and waited to see if the nearby Iraqi soldiers would react. None paid him any attention.

He pulled onto the coastal road. As he drove, he saw that several RPG rounds had struck the **Kuwait Towers**, though the damage was superficial—the iconic structures still stood.

Further along the Corniche, he saw soldiers everywhere. Tanks and armoured personnel carriers had ripped up paving stones, and sections of asphalt lay in chunks across the road. He drove slowly, dodging debris.

After about two kilometres, a group of Iraqi soldiers flagged him down. David rolled down his window, trying his best to appear calm. A man who appeared to be a **major** leaned into the car, staring at him with unsettling intensity. He didn't speak at first—just studied David's face.

Then, in perfect English, he asked, "Who are you, and where are you going?" David explained that he was a British national living nearby, opposite the Dasman Palace.

The soldier stepped closer, and David saw the man's eyes—old eyes, weary eyes, eyes that had seen far too much for a man barely 28 years of age. They chilled him. The major shifted a toothpick between his teeth and said in a low voice: "British... turn your car around. Go home. Do not come back here again."

David offered a half-salute, murmured, "Okay, you're the boss," and did exactly as he was told. Fortunately, he passed unhindered back to his building.

The State Security Building Falls
Later that morning, David witnessed a scene that would stay with him for the rest of his life.
Two enormous Iraqi helicopters hovered over the parking area next to the State Security Building. **Paratroopers slid down ropes**, landing swiftly and surrounding the facility.

From his vantage point, David could see over the perimeter wall. Inside, he saw several Kuwaiti security personnel stripping off their uniforms and changing into civilian clothes—trying desperately to escape capture.
They were not Iraqi soldiers. They were the men tasked with defending the State Security Building.

A tank shell had blown a hole in the wall. As an Iraqi soldier approached the opening, three Kuwaiti security officers—still in uniform—emerged with their hands raised in surrender. Not once did David witness any serious resistance.
It was a staggering confirmation of what the man with the Saddam moustache had said earlier:
"These Kuwaitis are like girls. Our guards will eat them..."
The invasion was swift, overwhelming, and brutally efficient.
And David—caught in the middle of it—now understood with complete clarity:
Kuwait had fallen.

The First Week
In the days immediately following the invasion, Kuwait descended into a strange mix of panic, silence, and disbelief. The city that David knew—busy, noisy, alive—became a place of shuttered shops, empty streets, and the steady rumble of armoured vehicles patrolling through every district. For expatriates, fear and uncertainty quickly turned into a quiet but urgent need to connect, to share information, and to survive.

During the first week, word spread quickly among the foreign workers living in Salmiya and other residential areas: **stay indoors**, keep a low profile, and avoid any confrontation or unnecessary movement. Phones lines worked intermittently, and the British Embassy had already been surrounded by Iraqi troops. There was no official guidance—only rumours and the instinct to huddle together.

Residents of David's building began gathering in the lobby or ground-floor lounge each morning, drawn together by anxiety and the need for news. Expatriates from Britain, the Philippines, India, Egypt, and elsewhere all found themselves in the same situation—cut off from their embassies, unsure what the Iraqis planned next. People traded whatever scraps of information they had:
- Someone had heard gunfire near the airport.
- Someone else claimed the Emir had fled.
- Another reported Iraqi soldiers looting government offices.

True or false, the rumours helped people process the reality that the Kuwait they knew had been overtaken in a matter of hours.

David became one of the calmest voices in the group—not because he felt calm, but because his practical nature gave others comfort. He encouraged people to conserve food, ration water in case utilities were damaged, and avoid drawing attention to themselves.

Planning Escape Routes
By the third day, small groups of expatriates began quietly discussing possible escape routes. The Iraqi Army had sealed off official borders and roadblocks were everywhere, but rumours spread of people trying:
- **The desert crossing into Saudi Arabia**, risky and nearly impossible without a guide.
- **The northern coastal road**, though most thought it suicide with Iraqi tanks stationed along every major route.
- **Fishing boats**, with some saying a handful of expats had attempted to reach Bahrain or Qatar under cover of night.

David listened but urged caution. The Iraqis had already begun arresting Kuwaitis at random, and anyone caught attempting to escape risked being detained—or worse. Still, the conversations continued in hushed tones, late at night, when the city settled under curfew and the only sounds were distant explosions or the clatter of tracked vehicles on asphalt.

Hiding and Making Themselves Invisible

Several expatriates, especially those from Western countries, took precautions to avoid being mistaken for government workers or military personnel:

- Some removed company logos from their vehicles.
- Others hid important documents—passports, visas, work permits—behind false panels or under floorboards.
- A few taped blankets over their windows to prevent silhouettes from being seen at night.

Women and children in some buildings stayed hidden in apartments for days at a time, too afraid to be seen by patrolling soldiers. Men took turns keeping watch from balconies or shadowed corridors, whispering updates whenever an Iraqi checkpoint appeared on the street below.

David himself remained indoors except for essential moments. When he absolutely had to move around the building, he did so cautiously, avoiding any sudden noise or behaviour that might attract attention. He also always kept a small bag ready—containing his passport, some cash, and essentials—just in case circumstances changed suddenly and he had to leave the building quickly.

A Community Bound by Fear and Solidarity

Despite the fear, something remarkable happened among the expatriates: a sense of solidarity grew. People who had barely spoken before now shared meals, radios, bottled water, even comfort.

Filipino housemaids prayed together in corners. Indian engineers exchanged theories on how long the occupation might last. British workers quietly discussed what the UK might do in response.

For David, the first week was an uneasy blend of waiting, listening, and staying alert. Every hour brought a new uncertainty. But amid chaos, the expatriate community formed a fragile network of mutual support—one that helped many get through the darkest and most unpredictable days of the occupation.

Shortly after the initial invasion, **David** went to a nearby residential tower to see whether he could make contact with other British or American nationals. The building, sixteen storeys high, housed several British families. In the reception area, he met a fellow Brit named **Bob,** team leader of a UK group responsible for the maintenance and operation of the Doha East Power Station.

Bob invited David upstairs to meet the others—families, children, technicians, all trapped in Kuwait with no clear understanding of what would come next. That evening they were gathering in one of the larger apartments for a communal meal, and they asked David to join them.

He returned later that night, and for a moment, it felt like stepping into a world untouched by war. They served turkey with all the trimmings. It was warm, comforting, and strangely celebratory amid the chaos outside. Some had wine, but David declined using his long-standing excuse: **"Thanks for the offer, but I'm allergic to alcohol."**

When he prepared to leave and return to his own building, he was strongly advised not to go—the Iraqi Army was patrolling continuously around their neighbourhood.

Instead, he was handed the keys to a fully equipped four-bedroom apartment. It belonged to a technician who happened to be on leave in the UK and would certainly not be returning under the circumstances. David accepted the offer of shelter; it was the only safe option.

For the next **six days**, he did not leave the building.

A Shocking Discovery

When David finally returned to his apartment in the other building, he was met with a shock. The place was **completely deserted**. No residents. No power. The elevators were dead, forcing him to climb six flights of stairs to reach his apartment

The door stood open.

Inside, chaos. The apartment had been **thoroughly ransacked**. All possessions were gone.

Drawers emptied, belongings stolen, and worst of all, thousands of cockroaches scuttling across floors and walls. The once-comfortable building had become, in less than a week, a filthy, uninhabitable shell. David had no choice but to relocate permanently to the other tower with the expatriate group.

Helping Each Other Survive

Food became a shared resource. The group pooled supplies and relied heavily on a few brave Indian friends who, despite the danger, were able to move more freely around Kuwait. These men risked their own safety repeatedly to bring food, water, and essential supplies.

One day, while hiding, David noticed blood in his urine and developed a high fever. He badly needed medical attention, but although the Amiri Hospital was within walking distance, the risk of being captured was too great.

One of the Indian friends stepped forward, went to the hospital, and returned with antibiotics and medication. David recovered because of these amazing people. Their loyalty and sacrifice left a lasting impression on him.

By contrast, attempts to obtain help from the British Embassy were deeply discouraging. Embassy staff were, in David's words, *clueless* and absent when needed. Senior staff seemed to have vanished. Only junior personnel remained, overwhelmed and lacking authority to act.

Whenever expatriates managed to reach the Embassy by phone, all they received was a pre-recorded message:

"Stay where you are and listen to the BBC for advice from the Foreign Office."

As David and many others later said, it was a disgrace.

The **Canadian Embassy**, on the other hand, was supportive, organised, and proactive—everything the British Embassy should have been.

Those in hiding agreed that if they ever got out, they would bring attention to the incompetence of the British mission. But once the conflict ended, public praise was lavished on the ambassador and others, effectively burying the truth of what had happened.

On **4th September 1990**, the Iraqi authorities unexpectedly permitted all women and children to leave Kuwait. It was heartbreaking to see families separated, but also a profound relief knowing they would soon be safe in the UK.

Living in Fear: The Mahabharata Raids Each day, the remaining expatriates met to discuss new information and their increasingly limited options. Movement was nearly impossible; Iraqi control over the country had tightened dramatically.

They lived in constant fear of the **Mahabharata**, Saddam Hussein's secret police. These men were notorious—lawless, violent, and accountable to no one. If they entered a building, people scattered into hiding places: inside air-conditioning ducts, behind false walls, or inside empty rooftop water tanks.

Everyone was terrified of them. A Mahabharata agent could kill without provocation and face no consequences.

Looters in the Tower

One day in September, loud noises from several floors below caught David's attention. Staying out of sight, he made his way down the stairwell. On the ground floor, he encountered a group of young Palestinian men carrying furniture and belongings from various apartments and loading everything onto a large flatbed truck.

One man lounged casually on an armchair in the lobby. David greeted him in traditional Arabic style and asked what was happening.

The man claimed they were taking possessions belonging to "friends." David knew this was a lie—the building housed only British technicians.

When challenged, the young man eventually admitted they were looting. "The residents have fled," he said. "They're not coming back. We can take what's left."

He explained, proudly, that **Kuwait was now the 19th province of Iraq**, and that Saddam Hussein had promised Yasser Arafat that Palestinians would become the top citizens in Kuwait, with Kuwaitis demoted to second-class status.

David pointed out that the international community would never accept Kuwait's annexation, and that UN forces were already mobilising.

The man grew angry. "Kuwait is Iraq now. Forever."

David couldn't help wondering whether this same group had ransacked his own apartment, stealing everything he owned—including his car. But in truth, looting was rampant, conducted by many different groups.

Not all Palestinians supported it, but many did—and some openly celebrated Iraq's occupation.

At the same time, trucks poured into Kuwait from Iraq daily, returning north **loaded with stolen goods**: electronics, refrigerators, furniture, cars, and even gold. The **gold souk was emptied**, and Kuwait's gold bullion reserves and international currencies were seized by Iraqi forces.

The Hidden Weeks and the Growing Danger

During the weeks David spent in hiding, everyone in the expatriate group found their own places within the building to disappear whenever Iraqi soldiers came through on their routine searches. Cupboards, crawl spaces, ceiling ducts, storage rooms—anything that offered concealment was used. Fear became part of the rhythm of daily life.

Then, on **4th October**, disaster struck. Two members of their hiding group were discovered and taken away by Iraqi forces. That evening, astonishingly, a phone call came from one of the captured men. He had been given access to a telephone under supervised conditions and delivered a chilling message.

One of the secret police officers had let slip that the **Kuwaiti resistance** was planning to kill some of the British expatriates in hiding and then blame the killings on the Iraqis. The aim, reportedly, was to provoke outrage in the UK and force the British government to take more decisive military action to liberate Kuwait.

The group was horrified—and the idea was shockingly plausible. They all knew how frustrated the resistance had become, especially as the UN continued to oppose military intervention at that stage.

An emergency meeting was held late into the night. Some argued that the safest course was to surrender to the Iraqis, believing that being taken into custody might be less dangerous than being targeted by resistance fighters. Others suggested relocating to a different building to reduce the risk.

David listened to all sides but held firm to his own view: **staying put was the safest choice.**

His reasoning was simple—the Iraqis had already caught two members of their group, but the rest had managed to remain hidden for weeks. He believed the story about the resistance was likely a fabricated psychological tactic designed to frighten them into surrender.

Despite his objections, the **majority voted to move** to a supposed safe house six miles away. David declined to go, and another man decided to remain with him.

The relocation was scheduled for **7th October**.

Chapter 11- Hostage

The Raid

But on **6th October**, before anyone could leave, their building was raided by the **Mukhabarat**, Saddam Hussein's secret police.

David managed to hide for a short time before he was discovered. In the end, every expatriate in the building—those planning to leave and those staying—was found.

They were all transported to the **Hyatt Regency Hotel**, which the Mukhabarat had converted into their headquarters. To their surprise, they were given generous meals—the best food they had eaten in weeks. The contrast between hospitality and terror was unnerving.

They spent one night there.

The following day, they were loaded onto a bus and taken on a long, tense journey across the desert to **Baghdad**.

Arrival in Baghdad and Transfer to Fallujah

Upon arrival in Baghdad, they were lodged overnight in the **Mansour Melia Hotel**, heavily guarded and surrounded by Iraqi security. The following evening, David was separated from the others and placed into a blacked-out Toyota 4WD.

For nearly two hours he was driven through unknown territory—no landmarks visible, no way to judge direction. When the vehicle finally stopped, he was escorted into what he later learned was **Fallujah**, where he would be kept as a *"guest" of Saddam Hussein's government.*

Life Inside the Industrial Facility

David's new "home" was a sprawling industrial complex—a factory purportedly producing chlorine, bleach, and similar chemical products. Yet beneath the surface lay something far more extraordinary.

The facility housed a massive **underground nuclear bomb shelter**, constructed by East German engineers. It was a hidden world of astonishing sophistication:

- Large, reinforced chambers

- Power generators

- Advanced air-filtration systems

- Water storage tanks

- A reverse osmosis plant

- Emergency provisions to support occupants for an extended period

The entrance was sealed by a huge circular steel door—the kind one might expect to see in a science fiction film.

This underground system had been designed to protect high-ranking personnel in the event of a nuclear attack.

Initially, David and the others were allowed access to explore this underground labyrinth. But once they began discussing the poor state of maintenance and pointing out obvious operational issues, access was abruptly forbidden.

Their sleeping quarters were in the administrative offices of the factory, complete with thin foam mattresses on the floor. There were **twelve hostages in total**, all foreign nationals, each coming to terms with the grim reality of captivity.

And so began a new and deeply unsettling chapter of David's ordeal.

Life inside the Fallujah industrial complex quickly settled into a strange, monotonous routine—equal parts boredom, fear, and constant uncertainty. The twelve hostages, including David, were confined to the administrative block of the factory. Their world shrank to a makeshift dormitory where they slept on a thin foam mattress on the concrete floor, a small common area, a basic bathroom, and that was it.

The day began at dawn when guards unlocked the doors. Meals were simple— rice, beans, flatbread, occasionally tinned meat. Sometimes fresh fruit appeared, but often, there was nothing more than a dented tin of something unrecognisable. Hygiene facilities were minimal, and showers were infrequent.

There was little to do. No newspapers. No radio. No contact with the outside world.

Conversation became the primary currency. The hostages exchanged stories of their lives, speculated endlessly about the progress of diplomatic negotiations, and tried to keep spirits up through humour, routine, and simple companionship.

But beneath every conversation lay the same unspoken thought: **No one knew how long they would be held—or whether they would be allowed to leave at all.**

At night, the silence was oppressive. The distant hum of machinery and the occasional rumble of trucks passing outside served as the only reminders that the world had not stopped.

Interactions with Guards and Other Captives

The guards were a mixture of Iraqi soldiers and intelligence personnel—some indifferent, others openly hostile. A few were surprisingly human, making small talk or offering cigarettes, curious about the Westerners now in their custody. Others wielded their authority with unpredictable aggression.

Most kept their distance, maintaining a rigid line between captor and captive.

David often found himself stepping into a quiet leadership role among the hostages. His calmness and ability to analyse situations helped reassure the others, especially during moments of tension when the guards barked orders or escorted individuals away for questioning.

The hostages formed a tight-knit group. There were engineers, technicians, administrators—men who had left families behind and were wrestling with fear, guilt, and homesickness. They supported each other through mealtimes, shared limited household chores, and watched over anyone who seemed close to breaking.

They learned quickly what topics to avoid around the guards—politics, the war, Saddam Hussein, and anything that might hint at criticism.

Even in captivity, survival was as much psychological as physical.

Julie's Experience and Fear Back in Scotland

Back in Scotland, Julie lived through those months in a state of relentless worry.

At first, she knew only that Kuwait had been invaded and that David was missing—possibly hiding, possibly captured, perhaps worse. Weeks went by with no reliable communication. Every news broadcast about Kuwait sent a chill through her. Every report of executions, hostage situations, or bombings added another layer of dread.

At one point the stress brought on a bout of Shingles which made her very ill at one point.

Scott tried his best to be strong for her, but he too was terrified. He went to school each day carrying a weight no child should have to bear, wondering if he would ever see his father again. Scott even had glandular fever which the doctor said was probably brough on by stress.

Julie wrote letters even though she knew David might never receive them. She spoke with other families of expatriates, clinging to the smallest pieces of information—rumours, embassy whispers, newspaper speculation. Nights were the hardest. Sleep came seldom and never stayed long.

She wrote letters to politicians, newspapers, even Margaret Thatcher, who replied to one of Julies appeals. The Bishop of Inverness even held a special service for David, Julie and Scott. She was going about the city posting yellow ribbons anywhere they could draw attention to the plight of the hostages.

Her greatest fear was not knowing. Not knowing whether David was alive. Not knowing whether he was suffering. Not knowing if she might one day receive a phone call that would shatter her life forever.

Yet she refused to give up hope. Every day she reminded herself: **"David is strong. He will come home."**

After months of captivity, international pressure mounted. The coalition against Iraq grew stronger, and Saddam Hussein—partly for propaganda, partly for political calculation—began releasing selected foreign hostages.

Word spread through the facility one cold morning that some of the men would be freed. David's name was on the list.

The relief was overwhelming, tempered only by a quiet guilt for the companions he would leave behind. He shook hands with each of them, offering words of encouragement. For many, his calm leadership had been a lifeline.

He was taken from Fallujah back to Baghdad, escorted through various checkpoints, and eventually turned over to diplomatic personnel. From there, arrangements were made for repatriation. The journey out of Iraq felt surreal— each mile carried him closer to safety and farther from the fear that had defined his life for months.

Finally, he boarded a plane bound for the UK.

When he stepped into the arrivals hall, exhausted and thinner than when he had left, Julie was waiting. She rushed into his arms before he could even speak.

David was home .Alive. Free. The nightmare was over—but the memory of those months would stay with him for the rest of his life.

Chapter 12- Home at last

Returning Home to Scotland

The following morning, **David, and Julie** boarded a flight to Inverness, returning at last to their home. Seeing **Scott** again brought a wave of relief and joy that David had scarcely allowed himself to imagine during captivity. And that first night, lying in his own bed beside his beloved Julie, he felt an overwhelming gratitude for the ordinary comforts he had once taken for granted.

Only now, after months of deprivation, did he fully realise how precious those simple things were.

David was noticeably underweight, and friends urged him to seek medical attention. He did so and was also offered counselling, which he politely declined. He felt no emotional trauma, no lingering fear. In his mind, he had been nothing more than a man caught in the wrong place at the wrong time. Life, he believed, throws unexpected hardships at all of us, and we survive them in whatever way we can.

He felt grateful—deeply grateful—to have come through the ordeal with his health and spirit largely intact.

For the first couple of weeks after returning home, David did little more than enjoy time with his family, attend AA meetings, and savour the simple miracle of being alive and unharmed.

Visits From MI6

During those weeks, David received two unexpected visits from men claiming to be from British Army Intelligence. It took little effort to realise they were **MI6**. They slipped up several times in conversation, revealing details no army intelligence officers would have had.

They questioned him extensively:

- about the Fallujah facility

- about the Mukhabarat's conduct

- about interrogation sessions with the Presidential Guard

- about the underground nuclear shelter and factory operations

But what surprised them most was David's perspective.

He told them plainly that he held **no bitterness** toward the Iraqi people. He believed he had been a victim of circumstance—caught in a geopolitical storm set in motion long before the invasion. He went further, pointing out that Western governments also bore a measure of responsibility for decades of instability across the Middle East. One of the MI6 officers tried to get him to retract those statements, but David insisted:

"Write it exactly as I say it. This is what I believe based on my own experience. Talking to Saddam would have achieved far more than bombing him."

He reminded them that Iraqi soldiers and staff had simply been doing their jobs—just as the two young intelligence officers had no choice but to travel to Inverness to question him.

They weren't unpleasant men—simply operatives carrying out their orders. After a second visit, they left him alone.

The only further contact came months later, on **18th January 1991**, when one of them called to inform him:

"The facility where you were held in Fallujah has been destroyed by RAF strikes."

David felt physically sick. He thought immediately of **Sloppy**, the dog that roamed the compound, and **Ali**, the man who had cooked for the hostages. He thought of Peter the Christian and Saad the Moslem, just two Iraqi lads who were the designated interpreters at the factory. But he knew he would never find out what became of them. The anger he felt surprised him—but it was real.

Julie's Quiet Strength

With life slowly returning to normal, David realised just how fortunate he had been—not only to survive captivity, but to come home to Julie. She revealed that although she had held power of attorney since their marriage, she had never once touched his bank account during the months he was held hostage.

When he asked her why she endured hardship unnecessarily, her answer was simple:

"I wanted to share the difficulties you were facing. I couldn't have lived comfortably while you were suffering. It wouldn't have felt right."

Such was the strength and character of Julie.

David also learned how lucky he was. Several men released from captivity returned home to find their marriages destroyed. One man discovered his wife had emptied his bank account and left with someone else.

David knew he had been blessed with a partner of remarkable loyalty and compassion.

Rebuilding His Life

He had lost a great deal of weight and needed time to regain his strength. After about six or seven weeks, once he felt physically ready, he made his way to the labour exchange to look for work.

A new chapter was beginning.

The Kuwait Liaison Group

Before David found new employment, he felt a strong need to reconnect with others who had endured the same nightmare. The shared experience of captivity had created an invisible bond between the former hostages—a bond few outside that circle could ever truly understand. And so, he reached out to several of the other British nationals who had also been held by the Iraqis.

Together, they formed a small support network which they named the **Kuwait Liaison Group**.

The group's purpose was simple: to bring people together, to share experiences, to compare notes, and to help one another process what had happened. Many had suffered far worse conditions than David, and some had been deeply affected emotionally. Others were simply desperate to talk to people who understood.

A decision was made to organise a gathering, not only for discussion but also for mutual comfort and solidarity. They chose a venue far removed from the desert heat and fear of Kuwait—a holiday camp owned by Pontins in **Blackpool**, a place synonymous with carefree leisure.

When the weekend finally arrived, around **forty-five people** attended. There were families, single men, women, and even children who had been caught up in the chaos of the invasion. Among them was **one man from the Fallujah group**—a reminder to David of the strange, dark chapter they had shared in captivity.

The reunion was emotional. There was laughter at shared absurdities, tears over painful memories, and long conversations that drifted between relief, anger, gratitude, and bewilderment. People compared their experiences of interrogation, hiding, evacuation, and the journey home. Those who had suffered more severe trauma found comfort in knowing they were no longer alone.

For David, the gathering cemented a sense of closure. It connected the loose threads of his experience, allowing him to place his ordeal in the broader context of others' suffering and resilience. It also showed him that while his own ordeal had been difficult, he had been far more fortunate than many.

The Kuwait Liaison Group continued to support each other in the months that followed, offering a sense of community that helped ease the transition back into normal life.

Soon afterward, David began preparing himself to re-enter the working world—carrying with him not only the lessons of captivity, but a renewed appreciation of freedom, family, and the fragile threads that hold life together.

In the weeks following his return home, **David** found himself unsure of what direction he wanted his life to take. The experience of captivity had changed him—not in ways that wounded him, but in ways that made him reassess what mattered. He knew he needed to work again, to rebuild his professional confidence and provide for Julie and Scott, but he wasn't certain where to begin.

As an intermediate step, he decided to apply for a government-backed employment scheme run by the **Labour Exchange in Inverness**. The programme was designed to give unemployed individuals access to tools that could help them seek work: computers, fax machines, telephones, postage supplies—everything necessary to conduct a proper job search.

Only a dozen people could participate at any given time. When David applied, he was told there was a **long waiting list**.

Most people would have accepted that. But David wasn't most people.

Determined, he went to the centre **every single day**, checking in with the manager, politely but relentlessly asking whether a space had opened. At first the manager brushed him off with the same weary answer, but David persisted—always courteous, always patient, but undeniably present.

Eventually, persistence won.

The manager, worn down by David's daily appearances and impressed by his determination, allowed him to enter the programme.

David threw himself into the opportunity. Every morning, he arrived as soon as the doors opened. Every afternoon he stayed until the centre closed. He wrote letters, typed CVs, prepared documents, and made speculative calls to companies across the UK and overseas. His focus was absolute—a man on a mission.

And then, just **six days** after joining the scheme, the phone rang.

It was **Costain**, one of Britain's major civil engineering contractors. They had a project starting immediately—an offshore **pipeline pull** in Middlesbrough—and needed someone experienced to work **back-to-back with another manager** aboard a barge called **the *Njord***. He would be a replacement for the existing manager who was ill. But he had to be prepared to start right away.

The terms were read to him over the telephone and a copy faxed to him. He went through it in 15 minutes and accepted it. The Costain HR manager dealing with it all told him a hire car would be sent to his home the following morning

The job was well paid. The work was technical, challenging, and exactly the sort of thing David excelled at.

He accepted without hesitation.

After months of captivity, uncertainty, and unemployment, David was heading back into the world he knew best—**marine construction**. It marked not only the beginning of a new chapter, but the return of David's professional identity, sharpened now by the resilience he had earned the hard way.

David left the facility early that day and eagerly went home to let Julie know he'd found work. After he had explained everything she felt more at ease. After all, Middleborough was not too far from Inverness.

The following morning, a car arrived from Hertz rental company and the keys handed over to David. He had packed his things and was ready to drive down to Middleborough.

David's First Days Aboard the *Njord*

When David arrived in Middlesbrough and first set eyes on the **Njord**, a heavy marine construction barge built for offshore operations, a familiar sense of purpose washed over him. The sharp smell of salt and diesel, the clang of steel underfoot, the controlled chaos of crews preparing equipment—these were the sounds and sensations of his old world. After everything that had happened in Kuwait, the Njord felt strangely reassuring. Solid. Predictable. Something he understood completely.

He met the man he was to work back-to-back with—a seasoned offshore superintendent who welcomed David with a firm handshake and a quiet nod of approval. Word of David's experience had already travelled. People on board seemed to recognise that he was someone who knew his trade, someone capable.

His first day was spent walking the deck, studying the layout of the equipment, reviewing the winch systems, anchor spreads, and the pipeline handling gear. The precise positioning of both barge and pipeline was supported by using a Decca Navigation System specifically adapted for this project.

He listened carefully to briefings from the barge master, the chief engineer, the diving team, and the tug skippers. It didn't take long before he was fully immersed in the operation.

By the end of the second day, David was already contributing suggestions— small improvements to rigging arrangements, anchor positioning, and safety procedures. His practical knowledge and calm authority impressed the crew, many of whom had worked with dozens of superintendents over the years. It was clear to them that David knew what he was doing.

For David, it felt good to be useful again.

The Pipeline Pull Operation and Its Challenges

The Njord acted as the primary platform to allow the pipeline to be precisely placed on the seabed in a pre-dredged trench. Using massive winches and a carefully arranged anchor pattern tension and alignment was achieved

The operation itself required precision, coordination, and constant vigilance. The pipeline, assembled in long welded strings offshore, had to be pulled on shore to its final resting position, guided carefully from the beach into deeper water.

Each string section was supported by large steel buoyancy tanks attached to the pipeline itself by wire tope slings. As the pipeline was pulled incrementally to its position it was allowed to be lowered into a pre-dredged trench on the seabed. When a section was in the precise position in the trench, divers would sever the slings. The buoyancy tanks would rapidly float to the surface and be retrieved by tugs standing by for this purpose. There were twenty-two divers onboard day and night for this important part of the operation.

The challenges began early.

1. Powerful Currents

The tidal currents off the Middlesbrough coast were stronger than expected. At certain stages, the pipeline wanted to drift off course, and David had to work closely with the anchor-handling tugs to maintain the barge's exact position. One wrong move, one anchor dragging, could kink or damage the pipeline.

His experience paid off. He directed repositioning operations calmly, giving clear, concise instructions that kept the pipeline perfectly aligned during the most critical stages.

2. Weather Windows

North Sea weather was unpredictable. A sudden squall or rising swell could halt the pull or cause dangerous strain on the pipeline. Weather forecasts were closely monitored, making the call to pause operations on more than one occasion.

These decisions weren't popular with everyone—especially those eager to finish the job—but they were necessary. And time proved him right each time; bad weather always arrived shortly after the pauses he ordered.

3. Mechanical Issues

Midway through the pull, the main generator began overheating. Without it, the entire operation would stall. David worked with the engineers to diagnose the issue. They discovered a failing hydraulic pump, and the repair required improvisation and speed.

Through teamwork and David's steady leadership, the winch was back online within hours—not days.

4. Coordination Between Teams

Pipeline pulls involve multiple specialised groups: divers, riggers, engineers, tug crews, surveyors, and onshore teams. Communication breakdowns can be disastrous.

David acted as the anchor point—literally and figuratively—bringing all teams together, ensuring everyone understood the plan, the hazards, and the contingencies. His ability to keep people focused under pressure won him respect across the entire project.

By the time the pipeline was fully installed and the operation complete, David had proven—both to himself and to the company—that he was not only back on his feet but performing at the top of his profession.

After months of captivity and fear, he had reclaimed something vital: his confidence, his competence, and the sense of purpose that had always driven him.

How Julie and Scott Adjusted to David Being Away Again

As David settled into his new offshore role on the *Njord*, life at home in Inverness entered a familiar yet emotionally challenging rhythm. Julie and Scott had endured long separations before, but this time felt different. What had happened in Kuwait still hung over the family like a shadow—not a dark one, but a reminder of how quickly life could change.

Julie tried to be strong as David left for his first rotation, but she couldn't help feeling a faint tremor of anxiety. Walking him to the door, watching him drive away—it stirred memories of the day Kuwait fell, memories she had spent months trying to soften with time.

Still, she carried herself with the quiet dignity that had always defined her. She knew David needed this work—not just financially, but emotionally. Returning to offshore operations helped him rebuild his confidence, reconnect with his profession, and reclaim the sense of purpose that captivity had threatened to erode.

And so, Julie adapted, just as she always had.

She kept busy with the home, her volunteer work, and staying connected to friends. The routines brought comfort. Evenings, though occasionally lonely, became easier to manage. She developed little traditions: a cup of tea as she listened to the late news, a phone call with Scott about his day at school, a letter or card she would put aside to give David when he came home.

She never said it aloud, but in her heart she felt relief each time David returned safely from offshore, relief wrapped in gratitude.

After Kuwait, every homecoming felt like a blessing.

For **Scott**, the adjustment was more practical than emotional. He understood, perhaps more deeply than most boys his age, that his father's work involved sacrifice. The fear he'd carried while David was missing in Kuwait lingered in small ways, but Scott had grown stronger for it.

He threw himself into school and social life. Football training, homework, and afternoons spent with friends kept him busy. On days when he missed his father more acutely, he would write notes or draw little sketches to show David when he returned. He liked having stories to tell: the goal he scored, the new friend he made, the subject he finally mastered.

Scott admired his father, and David's resilience after captivity became something of a private inspiration to him. Though he never said it, he was proud.

When David came home between rotations, the house filled with warmth and laughter in a way that was new—even brighter than before Kuwait. Simple things felt special:

- All three sitting around the table for dinner

- Julie watching father and son talk about football

- A stroll along the River Ness on a crisp morning

- Even the ordinary sound of David moving around the house

Every reunion reminded them how close they had come to losing this. And every farewell was softened by the knowledge that this time, David was safe, working in a world that made sense again—a world without soldiers, raids, or fear.

Little by little, the family healed.

Life did not return to exactly what it had been before Kuwait, but something quieter and more grateful took its place. The experience had reshaped their sense of what mattered, and in that way, it strengthened them.

Together, they learned to carry on—not by forgetting the past, but by living with deeper appreciation for the present.

Another Major Project Offer — A Return to Kuwait

After the successful completion of the *Njord* pipeline pull, David's reputation within the industry surged back to where it had once been. Word travelled quickly—Costain's senior management were impressed by his leadership offshore, his technical expertise, and his ability to stabilise operations under pressure. In a field where calmness and competence mattered more than anything, David had proven himself once again.

He returned home to Inverness for a few weeks of rest, grateful to settle back into family life. But just as he was beginning to wonder what his next assignment might be, the phone rang.

It was **Costain's regional director**, someone David had worked with years before.

"David," the man said with a tone of unmistakable intent, "we have something big lined up. Kuwait is commissioning major reconstruction works now that the country has been liberated. They need experienced people—people who understand the region, its challenges, and its politics. Your name came up immediately."

David felt a strange tightening in his chest. Kuwait.

The word alone conjured a torrent of memories—some terrifying, some bittersweet, some filled with faces he would never forget. The invasion, the hiding, the Mukhabarat raids, the captivity in Fallujah. Yet also the warmth of Kuwaitis he'd known, the beauty of the Gulf at sunrise, the friends who had risked their own safety to help him. The director continued.

"The project is large, one of the biggest marine reconstruction programmes in the Gulf. Ports are damaged, coastal defences are wrecked, dredging is desperately needed. Kuwait wants to rebuild fast, and they're asking specifically for engineers with local experience. We think you'd be perfect."

David didn't respond immediately.

His mind raced—logic, emotion, trauma, curiosity—all struggling for dominance.

Kuwait had changed dramatically in the months since liberation. Television broadcasts showed oil wells still burning, entire districts devastated, sea walls collapsed, and harbours filled with wreckage. Yet the Kuwaiti people were resolute, already planning for a future beyond the ashes.

And they needed men like David.

That night, David sat with Julie at the kitchen table and told her everything. She listened quietly, absorbing each detail, each possibility.

Her first reaction was instinctive—a tightening of her expression, the memory of the months of terror she had endured while he was held captive. A return to Kuwait, even a liberated Kuwait, triggered something deep within her.

But she also felt the weight of what the opportunity represented. David's experience in the Middle East, his understanding of marine construction, and his connections in Kuwait meant the offer was not random—it was earned.

"It's your decision," Julie said softly, placing her hand over his. "But if you go back… promise me you'll be careful. Truly careful. I don't want to live through another nightmare."

David nodded. He understood. More than that, he felt it.

Part of him longed to see Kuwait again—not the Kuwait of invasion, but the Kuwait he had known before, the country he had lived in with Julie and Scott, where Scott had gone to school, where they had walked on the Corniche, where they had built friendships across cultures.

Another part of him recoiled at the idea of stepping back into a place tied so closely to trauma.

After days of thought, discussions on contractual terms and conditions, reflection, and conversation, David contacted Costain. "I'll take it," he said. His voice was steady.

It was not a decision made lightly. It was not made without fear. But it was made with purpose.

Kuwait was rebuilding, and he felt compelled—not by pride, not by ambition, but by something deeper—to be part of that renewal. A chance to close a circle. A chance to confront the past not with fear, but with strength.

David had survived Kuwait at its darkest moment. Now he would return to serve it in its hour of hope.

Chapter 13- Arabia return

David's Arrival in Newly Liberated Kuwait

When David stepped off the aircraft at Kuwait International Airport, the heat struck him first—a dry, harsh blast so different from the heavy Gulf humidity he remembered. But it was what came next that truly made him pause. Silence.

Not the peaceful kind, but the aftermath-of-chaos kind. The airport, once bustling with expatriates, families, and business travellers, now bore the scars of occupation. Windows patched with plywood. Cracked tiles. Abandoned luggage trolleys rusting on the edges of the hall. Kuwait was free, but liberation had left its mark.

As David walked through the concourse, he felt a knot in his stomach. He had not set foot in Kuwait since the day he was taken to Baghdad months earlier. Returning now brought back memories of fear, hiding, and captivity—but also the good years before the war, the friends he'd made, and the life he and Julie had once built here.

A Costain representative met him outside the terminal and drove him into the city. The journey that followed was unlike anything David had ever seen. Kuwait City looked as though it had survived an apocalypse.

Much of the skyline remained recognisable, but everywhere he looked there were signs of destruction:

Government buildings burned out, windows shattered and blackened.

The Kuwait Towers charred, their once-bright mosaic tiles streaked with soot.

Traffic lights twisted or missing, replaced by soldiers directing vehicles through intersections. Entire streets lined with burned-out cars, some still bearing bullet holes. Residential districts looted, doors smashed, belongings scattered.

Most haunting of all were the oil fires. Even from miles away, great columns of thick black smoke rose into the sky like monstrous pillars. The smell of burning crude oil drifted across the city, clinging to everything. And during the day, the sun was often hidden behind dark clouds of smoke from the fires.

At night, he later learned, the horizon glowed red as hundreds of oil wells burned like torches in the desert—a sight both terrifying and unforgettable.

Yet amidst the devastation, there were signs of life and hope:

Kuwaiti flags flying from damaged buildings. Families clearing debris from their homes. Volunteers distributing water and supplies. Engineers and military convoys moving with purpose,

Shops opening with whatever stock they could find. Kuwait was wounded, but unbroken.

The Reconstruction Team

David's assignment was part of an enormous reconstruction programme. The team he joined was multinational and highly specialised, combining:

British and American marine engineers. Kuwaiti Ministry officials. Surveyors and dredging experts from Europe.

Local contractors urgently rebuilding coastal infrastructure. Environmental specialists, assessing damage from the oil spills and fires.

Security teams, because mines and unexploded ordnance still littered parts of the coastline.

Their base of operations was in a heavily damaged office building near the harbour, where generators roared all day and workers operated under cleaning lights because much of the electrical grid was still unreliable.

David's primary responsibility was to help restore damaged port facilities, repair breakwaters, and dredge channels choked with sand, debris, and sunken equipment. The Iraqi retreat had left harbours clogged with:

- destroyed ships
- vehicles
- dumped concrete blocks
- twisted rebar
- unexploded mines

The scale of the problem was staggering. It would take months—perhaps years—before Kuwait's ports functioned properly again.

But the team approached the work with a sense of mission. This wasn't just another project. It was a piece of Kuwait's future.

David found himself working with old acquaintances and new colleagues from across the world. There was a shared determination in the team—a quiet understanding that they were participating in something historic. They were building not just infrastructure, but stability, dignity, and recovery for an entire nation.

A Personal Turning Point

For David, being back in Kuwait was emotionally complex. Some days he felt strong and purposeful; others, he felt old fear stirring in the corners of his memory. But the work grounded him. The camaraderie reassured him. And witnessing the resilience of the Kuwaiti people reminded him why he had returned.

This was not the Kuwait he had fled in terror. This was a Kuwait rising again. And in his own way, David was helping it stand.

About six weeks into the reconstruction effort, David found himself facing one of the most dangerous challenges so far. The team had been tasked with clearing a heavily damaged portion of the breakwater near Shuwaikh Port—an area that had seen intense Iraqi activity during the occupation. Intelligence reports warned that Iraqi forces had mined several coastal structures before retreating, but no one knew exactly where the explosives had been placed.

Survey teams began scanning the seabed and the breakwater foundations using sonar and handheld detection gear. The results were alarming: the breakwater was riddled with metallic anomalies, some resembling submerged debris—others far more suspicious.

One morning, while David was organising the anchor spread for a dredger positioned close to the breakwater, a diver came up rapidly, signalling for urgent attention.

"We've found something that shouldn't be there," the diver said, breathing heavily.

It was a **Soviet-made anti-ship mine**, half-buried in the sand, entangled in broken concrete and rebar. One wrong movement from the dredger's anchors or suction head could trigger it. Worse still—there could be more.

David felt the weight of responsibility settle heavily on him. The dredger, crewed by more than twenty men, was working less than forty metres away. He made the decision immediately.

"Stop all operations. No one moves until we know exactly what we're dealing with." The team complied instantly.

A British EOD (Explosive Ordnance Disposal) unit was called in. For hours, David watched as they carefully probed the seabed, marking danger zones with floating buoys.

By the end of two days of intense and careful work, they had uncovered **three more mines**, each positioned to cause maximum damage to any vessel attempting reconstruction.

The EOD team later detonated the mines in a controlled blast offshore, sending a plume of water and smoke skyward.

For David, the incident reinforced a sobering truth: Kuwait's reconstruction wasn't merely an engineering challenge—it was a walk through the remnants of war.

But he also gained the profound respect of the crew. His decisiveness had protected dozens of lives and prevented a catastrophe that might have halted work for months.

Reconnecting

Despite the destruction and trauma that Kuwait had endured, the human spirit seemed remarkably resilient. Word spread quickly among those who knew David before the invasion that he had returned. Within days, familiar faces began to reappear.

One of the first was **Ahmed**, the young Kuwaiti soldier who had warned him on the night before the invasion that Iraqi troops were massing at the border. Ahmed was now back in Kuwait, discharged from military service after spending months as a captive by the Iraqis. He had been wounded in the foot and now had a pronounced limp, using a stick to get around

They met in a small café near Salmiya that had reopened only partially—half the chairs missing, scorch marks still visible on the walls.

Ahmed embraced him warmly. "You came back," he said, shaking his head with a mixture of disbelief and admiration. "Not many would."

David smiled. "Not many had unfinished business here."

They talked for hours. Ahmed recounted stories of how he was captured. David shared his own story—carefully, lightly, without dwelling on the darkest parts. Their shared history created a bond that carried them well beyond words.

Later that week, David also reconnected with **old colleagues from his pre-war projects**—Dutch surveyors, Filipino riggers, a Singaporean welder named Lim, and even a Kuwaiti engineer named Faisal who had once worked with him on the Amiri Diwan lagoon.

Faisal arrived at the office in a pristine white dishdasha despite the chaos outside and greeted David like a long-lost brother.

"My brother, you survived Saddam's prisons," he said, placing both hands on David's shoulders. "You must have an army of angels with you."

David laughed, but inside he felt a surge of emotion. Seeing these men—some thinner, some wearier, some with stories of loss—reminded him of the Kuwait he had once known. A place of warmth, humour, and cross-cultural camaraderie.

Reconnecting with them brought him healing he hadn't even realised he needed.

During the next twelve months, David oversaw several projects simultaneously for the company. During these months he was approached by other contractors who offered him employment opportunities.

He mulled the possibilities over the following months, and he eventually decided not to further renew his contract with Costain but to re-consider his future.

And then, the next thing on the agenda would be to take Julie and Scott for a luxury holiday in Cyprus and after that, a well-earned rest at home in Scotland.

David Returns to Scotland

David had barely settled into his armchair in Inverness when the phone rang. Julie handed it to him with a raised eyebrow.

"Another one of your admirers from Kuwait?" she teased.

David smiled and answered. "David speaking."

A warm, formal voice came through the line. "Mr. David, this is **Mohsen Al-Rashidi** calling from Kuwait. I hope you remember me."

David straightened. "Of course, Mr. Mohsen. We met during the reconstruction briefings. How are you?"

"Well," Mohsen replied, "alive, grateful, and rebuilding—much like our country. And that, Mr. David, is why I am calling."

David glanced at Julie, who was listening with quiet curiosity. "I'm on leave at the moment," he said, "but I'm happy to talk."

"Excellent," Mohsen said. "I will be direct. My company, **Mushreef**, has built roads, bridges, foundations. But Kuwait today needs more than roads. We must rebuild our ports, our coastal defences, our marine infrastructure. I wish to expand Mushreef into dredging and marine construction."

David leaned back. "You're entering a very competitive field."

"Yes," Mohsen replied calmly, "which is why I want the best man available. Someone with experience—not just technical knowledge, but someone who knows Kuwait, loves Kuwait, and understands the mentality of working here."

David paused. "And you think I'm that man?"

"Mr. David," Mohsen said with a soft laugh, "you survived Saddam's invasion, Iraqi captivity, and the reconstruction of our coastline. Who else would I choose?"

David glanced again at Julie, who mouthed: *Ask him the details.*

"All right, Mr. Mohsen," David said. "What exactly are you offering?"

Negotiation Begins

"We would like you," Mohsen said, "to establish and lead a **Marine & Dredging Division** within Mushreef. You will have full authority to hire staff, select and purchase equipment, and negotiate contracts—with board approval, of course."

"That's a big undertaking," David said. "You'll need vessels, pipelines, workshops, yard space, professional operators—"

"And you," Mohsen interjected gently. "Without the right leadership, equipment is useless."

David couldn't help smiling. "You're very persuasive."

"I am Kuwaiti," Mohsen replied. "We have been merchants since our grandfathers sailed to India in wooden dhows. Persuasion is in our blood."

David laughed. "Fair enough. What about the terms?"

"We will discuss everything properly when you come and visit us in Kuwait to see what our company has to offer.," Mohsen said.

"But I can tell you this: you will be well compensated. Villa accommodation, full medical coverage, car, annual business class family tickets, and a salary appropriate for someone building an entire new division."

"Competitive?" David asked.

"Very," Mohsen replied. "More competitive than you expect."

David hesitated. "Sounds very interesting Mr. Mohsen but I'll need time to consider it."

"Of course," Mohsen said. "Take one month. Speak with your wife. Speak with your son. If you say yes, we begin immediately. If you say no, I will respect it. But I hope," he added, "you will say yes. Kuwait knows your value."

There was a pause. "I appreciate the offer, Mr. Mohsen."

"And I appreciate that you answered the phone," Mohsen said warmly. "Enjoy your holiday. We will talk again soon."

The line went dead.

Julie folded her arms and studied David. "Well?"

He exhaled. "He wants me to start a marine division from scratch. In Kuwait."

Julie's expression softened—not fearful, but thoughtful. "That's a big responsibility."

"It is," David said.

"And a big opportunity," she added.

David nodded slowly. "Bigger than anything I've done before."

Julie stepped closer, resting a hand on his shoulder. "Whatever you decide… we'll face it together."

David looked out the window, the Scottish rain tapping gently against the glass. The future felt uncertain—but exciting.

A week after the first call, David received another telephone invitation from **Mr. Mohsen**, this time suggesting a formal discussion via faxed proposal and a scheduled follow-up call. By then, David had already been thinking deeply about the opportunity—its risks, its rewards, its weight. When the documents arrived, they were surprisingly detailed.

Later that evening, when the house was quiet, David read the proposal at the kitchen table while Julie prepared tea.

The Offer from Mushreef:

1. **Position:** *Director of Marine & Dredging Division.* Full authority to establish the division, recruit a core team, and manage all marine projects.

2. **Contract Duration:** Initially two years, renewable by mutual agreement.

3. **Compensation:**

4. High tax-free salary, significantly above his offshore rate.

5. Performance bonuses tied to project milestones.

6. Annual gratuity per Kuwaiti labour law

7. **Benefits:**

8. Company-provided villa accommodation in a secure expat compound

9.   Fully maintained 4x4 vehicle

10.   Business-class flights annually for the whole family

11.   Full medical insurance

12.   Established office, secretarial staff, and administrative support

13.   Authority to procure dredgers and marine equipment as needed

14.   **Start Date:** As soon as David was ready.

Julie read over his shoulder. She let out a low whistle.

"This is… generous," she said.

"It is," David replied. "More generous than I expected."

Then she turned his face gently toward her. "But is it what you want?"

He paused. "It's the biggest professional challenge I've ever been offered. And… I think I can do it."

She nodded. "Then we'll make it work."

The Family Decision

At the next family dinner, they discussed the offer more openly.

Scott, now on the brink of adulthood, listened thoughtfully.

"So, I'd stay here?" he asked.

"You'd start university," David said. "Edinburgh. A new chapter."

Scott nodded slowly. "I'll miss you both, but… I'll be okay. And Mum can go back and forth."

Julie smiled. "Every three months, I'll spend a month in Inverness. We won't abandon you, love."

Scott grinned. "I didn't think you would."

The decision, once spoken aloud, lifted something heavy from the room.

David Accepts

The next morning, David called Kuwait.

"Mr. Mohsen," he said, "I've discussed your offer with my family. I'm accepting."

There was a brief silence, then a warm, triumphant laugh.

"Mr. David, you have made me a very happy man. Kuwait will benefit greatly from your return."

They set a start date. Travel arrangements were made. A villa was allocated.

David hung up the phone and looked at Julie. "Well," he said quietly, "we're going back."

She kissed him lightly on the cheek. "Let's make it our best chapter yet."

Scott Starts University

The summer passed quickly. Scott received his acceptance to the **University of Edinburgh**, and soon the house was filled with lists, packing boxes, new clothes, and the slightly nervous excitement of a young man stepping into independence.

On move-in day, David and Julie walked him through the old stone quadrangles, helping him settle into student accommodation. Scott hugged them both tightly.

"Don't worry about me," he said. "Just don't get into any more wars."

David laughed. "I'll try."

A week later, David boarded his flight to Kuwait—returning once more to the country that had shaped so much of his life. But this time was different.

He was not returning as a hostage, nor as a man on emergency assignment. He was returning as a leader of a new division, with authority, purpose, and a company placing great trust in him.

When he stepped off the plane, he felt ready for the challenge.

Julie joined him two weeks later. They moved into a spacious villa in a quiet neighbourhood, furnished simply but comfortably. For the first time in years, they felt the thrill of starting something new together.

The plan was simple:

- **David** would work full-time building the Marine Division.

- **Julie** would stay with him most of the year, returning to Inverness every three months for a month to support Scott.

- **Scott**, now a university student, visited during holidays.

It was a rhythm that worked for all of them.

And as David drove through Kuwait City on his first morning with Mushreef, watching cranes rise and workers repair streets, he felt something he hadn't felt in a long time:

A sense of belonging. A sense of purpose. A sense of coming full circle.

The next chapter of his life had begun.

Chapter 14 - Mushreef

Building the Marine Division

The day David walked into Mushreef's headquarters for his first official meeting with the company board, he carried three things: a notebook, a clear vision, and the confidence that came from decades of marine construction experience. Mushreef had excellent credentials in road building and civil works, but when it came to dredging, coastal engineering, and offshore logistics, they were starting from zero.

David's mandate was simple in words but monumental in execution:

Build a fully operational Marine & Dredging Division—with vessels, crews, systems, and operational capacity—from scratch.

The board granted him an initial budget of seven million Kuwaiti dinars (**$22 million**) for capital purchases, crewing, mobilization, and administrative setup. It was generous, but not limitless. He'd need to spend every dollar wisely.

Preparing the Master Budget for Board Approval

David spent the first week gathering data, assessing project opportunities, studying Kuwait's dredging requirements, and mapping out the basics of what the new division would need.

In a detailed presentation to the board, he laid out:

Major Capital Purchases

1. **Two ocean-going tugboats** Essential for anchor handling, barge towing, logistics, and project support.

2. **One cutter suction dredger (CSD)** The heart of the operation— capable of channel dredging, reclamation, lagoon cutting, and pipeline trenching.

3. **A multipurpose survey vessel** for hydrographic surveys, positioning systems, crew transfers, and light towing.

4. **Support equipment** Floating pipelines, pontoons, anchors, winches, spares, consumables, and safety gear.

5. **Two 12m multi-cat** workboats fitted with 5t hydraulic Hiab cranes

6. **A 42-metre flat top barge** for general purpose use.

Personnel Requirements

-   Dredgemasters (3)

-   Tug masters (4)

-   Boat skippers (8)

-   Marine engineers (6)

-   Welders (4)

-   Fitters (4)

-   Surveyors (2)

-   Deckhands (16)

- Administrative and logistics staff (11)

Operating Expenses

- Mobilization costs

- Vessel registration

- Dry-docking and inspection

- Insurance

- Fuel

- Training and certifications

When David finished, Mohsen leaned back, tapping a pen against the table.

"You've built us a navy," he said with a grin.

David smiled. "A small one. But enough to get us into the game."

The board approved the budget unanimously.

Malaysia – Procuring Two Ocean-Going Tugboats

David's first trip was to **Malaysia**, where several reputable shipyards had ocean-capable tugs available for sale.

In **Port Klang Free Zone, Selangor, Malaysia** , he inspected five vessels. Two stood out immediately:

- **Tug 1:** A 3,000 HP boat with excellent bollard pull and recently refurbished engines

- **Tug 2:** A slightly smaller 1,800 HP tug with a strong maintenance history and excellent stability in shallow water

He walked the engine rooms, spoke with engineers, reviewed logbooks, and insisted on sea trials. The Malaysians appreciated his thoroughness.

During the sea trial of the larger tug, the captain turned to David and said:

"She's a workhorse, Mr. David. Treat her well and she'll never fail you."

David nodded. He already knew she was the right choice.

Both vessels were second hand, purchased for a negotiated price, and shipping arrangements were made to deliver them to Kuwait, this to be included in the purchase price.

Holland – Acquiring a Cutter Suction Dredger

Next, David flew to **Holland**, the global heart of dredging technology.

At the IHC shipyard near Rotterdam, he inspected a mid-sized **cutter suction dredger**—well-maintained, mechanically sound, and perfect for Kuwait's coastal conditions. The Dutch engineers demonstrated the cutter head, pump curve data, winch systems, and automated controls.

David spent hours reviewing performance logs and talking with the chief engineer. Everything checked out. The dredger had previously been in service with Bos Kalis but was now surplus to requirements and IHC were brokering the sale.

On the final day, the shipyard manager shook his hand.

"You will do good work with her," he said.

And David believed it.

Southampton – Purchasing a Survey Vessel

From Holland, David travelled to **Southampton** to inspect a survey vessel owned by Williams Shipping of Southampton a compact, versatile, and fast vessel with twin caterpillar engines It came equipped with:

- GPS positioning
- Echo sounders
- Side-scan sonar

- Small crane

- Cabin space for equipment and crew

It was ideal for pre- and post-dredge surveys, pipeline routing, and site assessments. After trials were done to assess performance levels and suitability for the hot climate of Kuwait, David approved the purchase. The vessel would be shipped to Kuwait within a month.

India and Singapore – Recruiting the Crews

Vessels alone were useless without trained men.

David travelled first to **India**, where he met with marine recruitment agencies and interviewed dozens of candidates. He looked for:

- Tug masters with coastal towing experience

- Marine engineers with diesel engine expertise

- Welders and fitters for dredger maintenance

- Deckhands accustomed to offshore conditions

He found excellent candidates—professional, experienced, and eager for Gulf contracts.

Next, he flew to **Singapore**, using recruiting agents to short list candidates. There he recruited:

- Surveyors

- Dredger operators

- Pipe welders and riggers

- Skilled mechanics

Singaporean and Indian crews had long been the backbone of Gulf marine operations. David knew how vital their skills were.

He conducted interviews personally, asking technical questions, reviewing certifications, and evaluating character.

He hired **a full complement of crew** for all vessels.

Back in Kuwait – A Division Takes Shape

When David returned to Kuwait, the office hummed with activity. Contracts were being typed, supply lists updated, accommodation arranged, medical checks completed. The first tugboat arrived in port to a small welcoming committee, including Mohsen, who beamed like a proud father.

"Mr. David," he said, "you are building something remarkable."

David nodded, though quietly he felt the weight of responsibility. There was still much to do—mobilization, training, sea trials, and preparing for Mushreef's first marine tender.

But for the first time, the Marine Division was **being constructed,** and David was the architect, the driving force behind its development.

The First Major Project

Barely three months after the new division became operational, Mushreef won its first major contract: **the rehabilitation and deepening of a coastal access channel leading to a new industrial facility south of Kuwait City**.

The scope included:

- Dredging a 3.5 km channel

- Deepening it from 4 metres to 8 metres

- Installing navigational markers

- Removing war debris left from the Iraqi occupation

- Rebuilding a small breakwater damaged during the invasion

Although modest compared to national mega-projects, this was a critical test for Mushreef. Success would establish credibility. Failure would sink the new division before it found its footing. David knew the stakes.

On the morning operations began, he stood on the deck of the cutter suction dredger, watching the tugboats position anchors. The survey vessel made passes across the planned trench line, logging seabed profiles. The newly recruited crew took their stations—men from India, Singapore, the Philippines, Pakistan, and a handful of new Kuwaiti trainees observing from the deck.

The dredger's cutter began to rotate, slowly at first, then with purpose. Sand and silt surged through the floating pipeline toward the reclamation area. The first day went smoothly. The second day did not.

The dredger encountered a submerged obstacle—likely remnants of war debris. Divers discovered a tangle of steel plating, twisted metal, and half-buried wire mesh. It could not simply be dredged; it required careful removal.

David coordinated the divers, tug masters, and deck crews as they extracted the debris piece by piece. It took two full days, but the operation resumed without damage to the equipment.

By week three, Mushreef began hitting excellent production rates. Client representatives, sceptical at first, started to express genuine admiration.

When the job finished, not only was the channel deeper than required, but it was completed **ahead of schedule** and **under budget**.

Mushreef's Marine Division, once an idea on paper, had proven itself.

Success did not come without challenges.

David's crew was multinational—highly skilled but culturally diverse. Men from different countries brought different habits, work rhythms, communication styles, and expectations.

Some of the challenges included:

1. Language Barriers

English was the lingua franca offshore, but not everyone had equal fluency. Instructions had to be given clearly and sometimes repeated several times. David made it a rule: **No one executes an order until they can repeat it back correctly.**

2. Work Culture Differences

Indian engineers tended toward precision and patience. Filipino deckhands excelled in teamwork and adaptability. Singaporean surveyors were methodical and disciplined. Pakistani riggers were strong, practical, and highly experienced.

But they had different approaches to hierarchy, decision-making, and safety practices. David spent hours each week holding briefings, encouraging questions, and building a culture of cooperation.

3. Introducing Kuwaiti Trainees

Some of the young Kuwaitis, having grown up after the invasion, lacked practical experience—and often had never worked offshore. For some, the long hours, heat, and physical demands came as a shock. The turnover of Kuwaiti recruits was very high. Many could not adapt to the hard work , long hours and strict timekeeping.

David knew the only way they would succeed was through patience, mentorship, and exposure.

David Mentoring Young Kuwaiti Engineers

David believed deeply in developing local talent. He remembered how Kuwaitis had supported him during his earlier years in the country, and he saw mentoring young engineers as a way of giving something back. And although the turnover of new Kuwaiti recruits was about 80%, David persevered with those who were trying hard.

His trainees included:

- **Faisal**, ambitious but inexperienced
- **Rashid**, quiet yet talented with technical drawings
- **Hamad**, who struggled at first but had grit

David's approach was simple:

1. **Explain the theory**
2. **Show them on the equipment**
3. **Let them try**

4. **Correct mistakes gently but firmly**

5. **Give responsibility bit by bit**

On one occasion, when a trainee hesitated during a dredge-line pressure reading, David placed a reassuring hand on his shoulder.

"Confidence," he said, "comes from understanding. Understanding comes from doing. Begin again."

The young man steadied himself, read the gauges correctly, and later said it was the moment he realised he was capable.

As months passed, the trainees began conducting surveys, assisting with anchor positioning, and even giving morning toolbox talks. David watched with pride as they transformed from cautious novices into confident marine engineers.

Word spread in Kuwait's engineering circles: **"If you want to learn real marine work, go train under Mr. David at Mushreef."**

The Marine Division was no longer an idea or an ambition.

It was a functioning, efficient, respected department—and David had become not just its leader, but its teacher, its architect, and its steady heart.

Julie's Life in Kuwait During This Period

While David was devoting himself to building Mushreef's Marine Division, **Julie** was quietly crafting a life of her own in Kuwait—one far more fulfilling than she had expected when she agreed to return.

Their villa in Salwa became her sanctuary. It was spacious, bright, and surrounded by neighbours from Britain, Canada, India, Lebanon, and South Africa. From her first week, Julie rediscovered something she'd missed deeply: a sense of community.

She sometimes accompanied David to the site office, not to involve herself in the engineering, but to understand his world and see firsthand all he was building.

She made friends easily. Kuwaiti women admired her gentle way of speaking and her curiosity about their customs. Expat women appreciated her honesty, steadiness, and the wisdom she had gained from years of living abroad.

Thursday evenings often meant small gatherings at friends' homes—potluck dinners, conversations that flowed into the night, and the kind of companionship that comes only from people living far from home and relying on each other.

On her days alone, Julie explored Kuwait's cultural side:

- browsing gold and textile shops in the Souk Al-Mubarakiya

- visiting the Tareq Rajab Museum

- enjoying early morning walks on the Corniche before the heat intensified

She had freedom, but she also had purpose.

Every few months she returned to Scotland for a month, spending treasured time with **Scott**, making sure he never felt forgotten or left behind. These visits became the heartbeat of her year.

Yet each time she boarded the flight back to Kuwait, she went with a sense of comfort—because David was there, because she now had friends waiting, and because, despite everything that had happened in the past, Kuwait felt familiar. Almost like a second home.

Scott flourished at university in Edinburgh.

The transition from Inverness Academy to the bustling academic world of a major Scottish university was challenging at first, but Scott adapted quickly. He threw himself into his studies—motivated not only by natural curiosity but also by a quiet determination to make his parents proud, especially after everything the family had endured.

He joined a few university societies, made friends from different countries, and even enjoyed the independence of managing his own small flat near campus. His lecturers found him diligent, thoughtful, and unusually mature for his age.

Every holiday, he flew out to Kuwait.

His first visit left him astonished. He remembered Kuwait as a child—sunny, vibrant, easy. Now he saw the reconstruction, the cranes along the skyline, the endless activity in the port and industrial zones. And he saw **his father**, not as just "Dad," but as a respected leader in a major engineering company.

David would take him to project sites—carefully, safely—and explain the work:

"This is the cutter head," "These are the survey grid points," "This is how the anchor pattern holds position," "This is the new channel we're cutting."

Scott listened, fascinated.

Evenings were spent with Julie and David eating at small restaurants in Salmiya, strolling through the old souk, or relaxing in the villa with movies and conversation. Occasionally, Scott joined David's colleagues for barbecues or football matches on the compound's pitch.

Kuwait broadened him. University matured him. The combination strengthened his confidence in ways nothing else could.

And every time he flew back to Edinburgh, he carried a renewed sense of connection to both his parents and to Kuwait—a place that had shaped his childhood and continued to shape his perspective.

Part-Time Studies

Despite the demanding workload of running Mushreef's Marine Division, David felt a growing desire to deepen his academic foundation. Though his decades of hands-on experience were immense, he wanted the formal education to match the depth of his practical knowledge.

So, over the course of three years, he enrolled in a **part-time engineering programme at Kuwait University**.

It wasn't easy.

His days were spent at the yard, onboard tugs, in meetings, and surveying sites. His evenings—often when others were relaxing—were devoted to lectures, textbooks, and assignments. Julie admired his determination; even after long hours in the heat, David would sit at the dining table with his spectacles on, scribbling diagrams of dredging hydraulics, soil mechanics, fluid dynamics, and marine construction methods.

The programme revitalised him intellectually.

He discovered he enjoyed academic work just as much as field operations—though in a different way. The technical rigour, the challenge of solving complex problems, the satisfaction of connecting theory with decades of practical experience...it all clicked.

By the time he earned his qualifications, David had not only expanded his knowledge but also earned the respect of the university's faculty.

Meeting Professor Archie Sherbourne

It was during his second year at Kuwait University that David met **Professor Archie Sherbourne**, a distinguished academic from the **University of Waterloo in Ontario, Canada**, one of the leading engineering faculties in North America. Archie was on a one-year sabbatical, teaching advanced structural and marine engineering courses.

Archie was a tall, silver-haired man with a lively sense of humour and the easy confidence of someone who had spent decades navigating the halls of academia. He and David connected almost instantly.

What began as after-class discussions about dredging techniques and coastal infrastructure soon developed into a genuine friendship. They often met at a small café near the university, where they talked about:

- engineering challenges

- life in the Middle East

- global maritime practices

- academic research

- and occasionally, just the absurdities of life

Archie was fascinated by David's career. "You've done the work most academics only write about," he told him one afternoon. "You've lived it— machine failures, tide changes, deep-water challenges, multinational crews. You've managed the human element. That's rare."

David laughed. "I just did the job that needed doing."

Archie shook his head. "You don't give yourself enough credit. Very few engineers can translate field knowledge into teaching. You could."

About six months into their friendship, Archie made a remark that would stay with David long after the moment passed.

They were sharing tea after a lecture when Archie leaned back and studied him thoughtfully.

"David," he said, "have you ever considered living in Canada?"

David raised an eyebrow. "Canada? Me?"

"Why not?" Archie replied. "Your knowledge of marine construction is exceptional. You've managed large teams, complex logistics, and high-risk operations. You've lived on tugs, barges, dredgers—and you understand them better than most people I've worked with."

David shrugged. "I'm not exactly the academic type."

"Rubbish," Archie said. "You'd be brilliant. You could teach marine engineering—dredging principles, offshore logistics, coastal development. Waterloo or one of our technical institutes would snap you up. You have what we look for: real-world depth."

David didn't know what to say. Part of him felt flattered. Another part felt overwhelmed. Canada? Teaching?

Archie saw the hesitation.

"Think about it," he said gently. "A quieter life…a new start…a chance to shape young engineers with your experience. You'd do very, very well."

David carried that thought with him long after Archie returned to Ontario.

Though he loved his work in Kuwait, Archie had planted a seed—one that would take years to grow but would slowly reshape David's sense of what might be possible for his future.

Julie's Life in Kuwait – Friendship, Culture, and Belonging

During the years David built the Marine Division and attended university, Julie's own world in Kuwait grew richer and more fulfilling than she ever expected.

It all began when she met **Nada and Huda**, two sisters from Bahrain who had married into a prominent Kuwaiti family. Julie first met Nada at a women's brunch, and the two immediately warmed to each other.

Nada was refined yet down-to-earth, with a sharp wit that reminded Julie of her friends back home. Huda, outspoken but equally warm, quickly became part of the growing bond.

Soon Julie found herself invited regularly to their family gatherings—events steeped in tradition, generosity, and incredible hospitality.

She learned their customs:

- the etiquette of greeting elders

- the meaning of the colourful abaya's worn at women's gatherings

- how family lineage shaped social relationships

- the deep emotional ties Bahrainis maintained with Kuwait

The sisters took her under their wing, introducing her to *their* world within Kuwait—a world most expatriates rarely experienced. Julie found herself welcomed with genuine affection by the extended family: mothers, sisters-in-law, cousins, even the elderly matriarch who spoke little English but communicated warmth with her eyes.

Julie attended *Ghabgas* during Ramadan, weddings filled with music and dazzling dresses, and family lunches that lasted entire afternoons. She learned to appreciate Arabic coffee served in tiny cups, cardamom sweets, and the beautiful ritual of women coming together to talk about life, marriage, children, and the future.

For the first time, Julie didn't feel like a temporary resident in Kuwait. She felt rooted. She felt connected. She felt at home.

Her friendship with Nada and Huda became one of the most meaningful relationships of her life—deep, steady, and full of laughter. These women, so different in culture yet so similar in heart, became amongst her closest companions during her years in the Gulf.

Scott's Graduation and Ambitious Early Career

While Julie's world blossomed in Kuwait, **Scott** was thriving in Edinburgh.

Years of disciplined study, independence, and the broadening experience of university life had shaped him into a confident young man. When graduation day arrived, David and Julie flew from Kuwait to attend the ceremony. Sitting in the hall, watching their son cross the stage in cap and gown, David felt a profound swell of pride—one of the purest moments of fatherhood.

His First-class degree in Business Administration was presented to him by the right honourable Malcolm Rikind who was at the time Foreign Secretary in the Conservative Government. After earning his degree, Scott surprised no one when he said: "I want to go into banking.

He had always been analytical, sharp, and ambitious. But then he added something that *did* surprise them: "My goal is Goldman Sachs on Wall Street. I want to work in New York. My plan is to be accepted in less than three years from now.

David raised an eyebrow. Julie blinked. But Scott's eyes were steady. He explained his plan with clarity:

- Start with a graduate programme in a major UK bank.

- Gain expertise in financial markets, risk management, and investment strategy.

- Build a competitive CV.

- After no more than three years, apply for a transfer or a role in New York.

He was determined—not impulsively, but with a strategic mindset.

Julie felt a mixture of pride and motherly concern. New York was far... and big... and intense. But Scott had always shown resilience. If anyone could carve a niche in the financial markets, it was him.

David listened carefully, then smiled and said: "Set your course and go for it, son. Just like a ship leaving harbour—know your destination, keep correcting your heading, and you'll get there."

Scott's journey began in Edinburgh, where he quickly secured a place in a prominent bank's graduate analyst programme. His natural ability with numbers, combined with a keen instinct for market trends, made him stand out early.

He embraced the long hours, the fast pace, the constant pressure—because to him, it wasn't pressure; it was the path to his dream.

And every holiday, he still flew to Kuwait to visit David and Julie—bringing tales of market movements, and a spark in his eye that only ambition can ignite.

David had a surprise one day when a friend sent him a cutting from the Financial Times of London. There was a short write up on Scott, congratulating him on being nominated as **Young Scottish Banker of the Year.** And Scott had not even mentioned it.

In his first year, he'd added a truly significant addition to his CV.

He felt so proud of his son.

Julie and David Discussing Their Future as Scott's Career Takes Off

As Scott's career in London began to gather momentum, Julie and David found themselves entering a new stage of life—one that felt both exciting and uncertain. Their son was no longer a boy navigating school or university; he was a young professional carving out a place in the ruthless world of finance, moving with purpose toward Wall Street.

Back in Kuwait, the villa felt quieter than before. Scott's visits grew shorter and less frequent as his responsibilities increased. His phone calls were enthusiastic but brief, filled with talk of markets, hedge funds, foreign exchanges, and the demanding rhythm of high finance.

One evening, after a dinner at the Sheraton with friends, Julie and David sat on the balcony overlooking the calm Gulf waters. The sky glowed deep orange as the sun dipped below the horizon.

Julie rested her hand on David's arm. "He's really finding his way, isn't he?"

David nodded, a soft smile on his face. "Yes, he is. He's got focus. Ambition. More drive than I ever had at his age."

Julie laughed gently. "Not more drive—just a different direction." They sat quietly for a moment, each lost in thought.

Then Julie said, "David... what about us? Our future. Have you thought much about it lately?"

David leaned back in his chair, exhaling slowly. "I have, my darling. More than you might think."

She looked at him, encouraging him to continue.

"You know," he said, "we've spent most of our lives moving forward to the next job, the next project... one challenge after another. Now Scott's off on his own path. He's strong enough to find his way without us hovering."

Julie smiled. "I suppose that's what makes me proud—and a little bit sad."

"He'll always need us," David said softly. "But in a different way now."

Julie nodded. "So, what do we want, David? A few more years here? Or something different?"

David took a long moment before answering.

"Kuwait's been good to us," he said quietly. "It gave us work, purpose, friendships, and a life we never expected. But we won't be here forever. There'll come a time when we'll want to slow down... maybe even move closer to Scott. Or somewhere peaceful. Somewhere we can breathe."

Julie's expression softened. "You're thinking about Canada, aren't you? Archie Sherbourne has been in your ear."

David chuckled. "He has, that's true. He thinks I'd do well teaching. And part of me wonders what that life would be like—less chaos, more reflection. Maybe passing on what I've learned."

"And what do *you* think?" Julie asked.

David turned to her, his face thoughtful. "I think... for the first time in years, our options are wide open. We're not tied to anything. We could stay here, or move to Scotland, or even try Canada. Wherever we go next, I just want us to face it together."

Julie squeezed his hand. "That's all I want too."

The warm breeze swept across the balcony as they sat quietly, the lights of Kuwait City shimmering in the distance. The future felt lighter than before— uncertain, yes, but full of possibility. They had spent so many years fighting through crisis, rebuilding their lives, and adapting to every twist of fate. Now, as Scott pursued his dreams and David and Julie contemplated their own, a sense of peace settled over them. Whatever came next, they knew they would meet it side by side.

Chapter 15 – A new Interest

David's First Computer

In **1993**, while Kuwait continued rebuilding and David's role at Mushreef grew more demanding, another transformation was quietly beginning—one that would change his working life - forever.

It started with a **second-hand Sony laptop**, a sturdy, boxy machine running on **MS-DOS**. David bought it from a British engineer who was leaving Kuwait. The price was high, but to David, it felt like stepping into the future.

He brought the laptop home and set it carefully on the dining table. Julie looked at it with mild suspicion.

"Are you sure that thing won't explode?" she joked.

David laughed. "If it does, it'll be my own fault for pressing the wrong button."

The truth was, he was completely new to computers. But David had never been intimidated by engines, machinery, hydraulics, or offshore operations—and he approached the laptop with the same determination.

David bought a stack of books from the small computer shop in Salmiya:

- **DOS for Beginners.**

- **Lotus 1-2-3 Spreadsheet Guide.**

- **Understanding Modems.**

- **Introduction to the Internet.**

Every evening, after work, he sat with the Sony laptop and his books spread across the table, teaching himself line by line:

- **how to navigate directories.**

- **how to write simple commands.**

- **how to load programmes.**

- **how to correct system errors.**

When he successfully typed a DOS command without crashing the machine, he felt an absurd but sincere sense of triumph.

Discovering the Internet

Then came the modem.

When he plugged it in and heard the strange symphony of beeps, clicks, and hisses as it connected, he sat in awe. It was like listening to a machine speak its own secret language.

His **first email**, sent to a colleague in the UK, was only one sentence long:

"Testing… please confirm you receive this."

When the reply came minutes later—

"Got it. Welcome to the future." David felt a thrill he hadn't experienced since steering his first dredger decades earlier.

The idea that he could communicate instantly across the world felt miraculous. He became absorbed.

Julie would walk past the table and shake her head affectionately. "You've become a computer addict," she teased. But she also knew how much joy it brought him.

Putting Technology to Work

Before long, David began exploring how the computer could enhance his work at Mushreef.

He mastered early spreadsheet software (Lotus 1-2-3, then later Excel) and realised he could:

- calculate production rates

- track budgets

- forecast dredging cycles

- build financial models

- create mobilization schedules

Tasks that once took hours with calculators and paperwork now took minutes.

He taught himself word-processing applications and soon began typing:

- tenders

- method statements

- equipment lists

- cost analyses

- project schedules

Instead of handwritten or typewriter-drafted submissions, David now produced professional, clean, organised documents that impressed the clients.

The real breakthrough came when he discovered **Primavera**, one of the earliest and most powerful project scheduling tools used in construction.

At first the interface was intimidating—Gantt charts, dependencies, resource loading, critical paths—but David persevered. He read manuals, experimented, made mistakes, corrected them, and finally mastered the software.

Primavera became his secret weapon.

With it, he could:

- plan entire dredging operations

- link tasks by dependencies

- forecast project delays

- allocate manpower intelligently

- show clients exactly how long each phase would take

It elevated his professionalism to a new level.

A Quiet Revolution. Within a year, David went from being a man who had never touched a computer to one of the most technologically capable managers in the company.

His colleagues were impressed. Mohsen was delighted, and David himself felt invigorated.

In a way, the laptop became more than a machine. It was a symbol of resilience. Of evolution. Of a man who refused to stop learning—no matter his age. This new skillset would later open doors he never expected.

A Client Presentation That Changed Everything

By early 1994, David's mastery of spreadsheets, word processing, and Primavera scheduling had become an asset not just for Mushreef's Marine Division—but for the entire company. Until then, most contractors in Kuwait were still presenting bids in the old-fashioned way: printed pages, hand-drawn sketches, and rough timelines typed on office typewriters.

David was about to change that.

The High-Stakes Tender

Mushreef had been shortlisted for a **major marine infrastructure project**, a contract issued by a powerful government ministry with close ties to the Amiri Diwan. Winning it would elevate the company's marine division and secure years of steady work.

The final stage of the tender process involved an in-person technical presentation before a panel of government officials, engineers, and financial auditors.

Mohsen called David into his office.

"Mr. David," he said, "this is our chance. Prepare whatever you need. Show them what we can do."

David nodded. "Leave it with me."

Preparing the Presentation

That night, David sat at his laptop for hours, building a detailed technical package:

- **A Primavera schedule** showing every phase of dredging, mobilization, and construction over twelve months

- **Spreadsheet cost models** broken into labour, equipment, overheads, and contingencies

- **Graphics and diagrams** created digitally - rare at that time in Kuwait

- **Production forecasts** plotted through charts

- **A cash flow projection** tied directly into the schedule

For visuals, he even added simple digital renderings of anchor patterns, pipeline routes, and cutter swing arcs.

Julie watched him from the sofa, smiling proudly. "It looks like you're planning the moon landing," she teased.

He grinned. "In Kuwait, a good dredging project is harder."

Presentation Day

At the ministry headquarters, the boardroom was filled with men in immaculate dishdashas, senior engineers with thick binders, and government officials known for their sharp scrutiny. Mushreef was one of several competing contractors, some international.

When it was David's turn, Mohsen introduced him warmly:

"This is Mr. David—our Marine Division Director. He will explain our methodology and schedule."

David stood confidently, placed the laptop on the projector tray (a novelty in itself), and opened the first slide. A crisp digital timeline filled the screen.

There was a murmur around the room.

Government officials leaned forward. Ministry engineers whispered to each other. One of the senior officials adjusted his spectacles and stared more intently.

No other contractor submitting a tender for the works had presented anything like this.

The Turning Point

David walked them through the plan:

- Each dredging phase linked by dependencies
- Weather contingency buffers
- Anchor spread configurations
- Cutter capacity and output rates
- Cost analysis tied directly to productivity
- Manpower schedules matched to the critical path

He clicked to the next section: **a live Primavera demonstration**. The room fell silent.

When he changed a single activity duration and the entire timeline recalculated instantly, one of the ministry engineers gasped softly:

"Subhan Allah... it updates by itself."

Another leaned toward David. "This is... American software?"

"Primavera," David replied with a smile. "Project management. Every number is connected."

They asked dozens of questions. David answered each with precision.

Then came the moment that sealed it.

An official asked: "If weather or equipment delay occurs early in the project, how do we see the impact?"

David nodded. He made a small change on the schedule.

The Gantt chart updated. The cost projections recalculated. The completion date shifted automatically.

The entire panel watched in awe. One senior official finally said: "Gentlemen... Mushreef is a Kuwaiti contractor who can show us the future before it happens." Mohsen nearly burst with pride.

After the meeting as they walked out, Mohsen clapped David on the back.

"Mr. David... you have just changed the way Kuwait does engineering." Two days later, Mushreef received the official letter:

THE CONTRACT IS AWARDED TO MUSHREEF.

It was one of the proudest moments of David's career. Not because of the contract's size—but because he won it not with muscle, machinery, or manpower......but with knowledge.

Beginning with a second-hand Sony laptop and the determination to learn David had given Mushreef an edge no one expected.

And it would not be the last time.

Chapter 16 – Canada

By **1998**, after nearly a decade of service, David had brought Mushreef's Marine Division to a level no one could have imagined when it began. The division had modern vessels, a trained multinational workforce, and a reputation for reliability and precision. He had overseen major contracts, navigated political complexities, trained young Kuwaiti engineers, and helped rebuild a country emerging from the trauma of occupation.

But David also sensed that his time in Kuwait was drawing to a natural close.

The long hours, constant heat, and unrelenting pace had taken their toll. And with Scott now firmly establishing himself in the world of banking—his eyes set on London or even Wall Street—David and Julie began to wonder whether it was time for a new adventure.

The idea of remaining in Kuwait indefinitely no longer felt right.

With a solid financial foundation, strong savings, and professional accomplishments behind him, David made a quiet and confident decision:

He would leave Mushreef and begin a new chapter—on his own terms.

Reconnecting with an Old Friend

Not long after leaving the company, David reached out to his old friend **Professor Archie Sherbourne** in Canada. Archie had always told him:

"David, you'd fit in beautifully in Canada. You could teach. You could build a life here."

Archie's invitation had been open for years, and now the timing felt perfect.

So David and Julie packed their bags and travelled to **Waterloo, Ontario**, where they were welcomed warmly into the Sherbourne household. It was summer—long daylight hours, warm evenings, green lawns, and the gentle rhythm of Canadian life. Julie fell in love instantly.

Waterloo was peaceful, orderly, friendly—and the opposite of the frenetic energy of Kuwait City. The people greeted them easily, conversations flowed naturally, and the sense of community reminded Julie of Scotland, yet with a new-world openness.

David, meanwhile, found himself fascinated by the engineering faculty at **the University of Waterloo**, one of the most respected in Canada. Archie arranged for him to visit the campus, sit in on classes, meet other professors, and even give a short informal talk on dredging operations in the Persian Gulf.

The faculty were enthralled. "Your field experience is extraordinary," one professor told him afterward. "We have students who would learn more from one semester with you than from an entire year of textbooks."

The Dean of Engineering—after a long conversation in his office—asked the question outright: "Mr. Bentley... would you consider joining our faculty as a lecturer?"

David blinked. Julie squeezed his hand. Archie grinned knowingly.

The idea that had once been a distant seed—planted long ago during their talks in Kuwait—had suddenly blossomed into a real opportunity.

Making the Decision

That evening, David and Julie took a long walk through Waterloo Park. The air was cool, the lake still, families were feeding ducks, and young couples held hands on the footpaths.

Julie looked up at David. "Well?" she asked. "What do you think?"

"I think," he said slowly, "that this could be the fresh start we've been waiting for."

Julie nodded. "It feels right. Safe. Peaceful. And Scott is only a seven-hour flight away in London. We could build a life here, David."

They sat together on a bench, watching the sun set through the trees.

David whispered, almost to himself, "Teaching... a new purpose. A chance to shape the next generation. After everything we've lived through... maybe it's time."

Julie took his hand. "Then let's do it."

The First Step – Renting a Home

Before returning to Kuwait to pack their belongings, David and Julie spent several weeks in Waterloo making practical arrangements.

Archie helped them find a small, charming **rental house on a quiet street** not far from the university. It had:

- a wide front porch

- maple trees lining the sidewalk

- a bright living room

- and a spare room where David could set up an office

Julie visited local shops, grocery stores, and cafés—testing the rhythm of daily life. She made friends quickly with neighbours who were curious about the Scottish Kuwaiti couple moving in next door.

By the end of the two months, both David and Julie felt it:

Canada wasn't just an option. It was their future.

They flew back to Kuwait with a sense of peace—and a sense of purpose. A new chapter was waiting for them across the Atlantic.

Their Final Months in Kuwait

Once the decision to move to Canada was made, the final months in Kuwait took on a bittersweet tone. The dust-coloured city that had once been a battleground, then a construction site, had become their home. Every street held memories— from the old Corniche where they used to walk in the cooler months, to the bustling souks Julie visited with Nada and Huda.

Julie struggled quietly with the idea of leaving her closest friends in the Gulf. Nada and Huda, who had become like sisters to her, invited her to countless gatherings—all filled with laughter, gifts, food, and affectionate teasing.

"You will come back to visit," Nada insisted, her eyes welling up. "You cannot disappear into the snow forever!"

Julie hugged her tightly. "I'll come back. I promise."

David, meanwhile, made rounds at Mushreef, not for business but to say his farewells. The engineers he had trained and mentored lined up to shake his hand. Many spoke from the heart:

"You changed this division. You were like a father to us. We will never forget how you treated us."

Even Mohsen, a formal man who rarely showed emotion, embraced David before he left the office for the last time.

"Kuwait is better because you were here," he said quietly.

For David, it was one of the greatest compliments of his life.

Preparing to relocate to Canada was a logistical marathon.

A freight company came to pack their household items:

- David's treasured books and engineering papers
- Julie's collection of Middle Eastern crafts and gifts

- A few pieces of furniture

- Clothing suited for warmer climates (though Julie insisted they would need entirely new wardrobes for Canadian winters!)

Watching the boxes sealed and loaded into the container felt like sealing a chapter of their lives.

Immigration Paperwork

Archie guided David through the complex Canadian immigration process:

- Employment verification from the University of Waterloo

- Medical examinations

- Proof of savings

- Criminal checks

- Sponsorship documents

- Temporary work permits transitioning into permanent residence

It took patience—and a few anxious weeks—but eventually everything was approved.

The day the visa documents arrived, Julie held them in her hands like precious certificates. "It's real now," she whispered. "We're really doing this."

David's First Semester

David began his first semester with a mixture of excitement and humility. Teaching was a new world—structured, intellectual, and steady—nothing like the unpredictable urgency of marine construction.

He taught courses in:

- Marine Engineering Fundamentals

- Dredging Operations

- Coastal Infrastructure

- Project Management with Primavera

Students quickly discovered that this was no ordinary lecturer. David brought the field into the classroom:

- Photos from Kuwait

- Real dredging logs

- Case studies of the Amiri Diwan lagoon

- Hydrographic charts from the pipelines he'd laid

- Tales of offshore storms, breakdowns, and narrow escapes

He didn't just teach engineering. He taught experience.

Students respected him deeply—many saw him as a mentor. Some lingered after class to ask questions; others invited him to coffee to hear more about life in the Middle East. By mid-semester, the department chair congratulated him:

"We've never had this level of engagement in marine courses. Whatever you're doing—keep doing it."

Julie Settling In

Julie blossomed in Canada almost immediately.

She loved:

- the friendliness of neighbours

- the quiet streets

- the maple trees changing colours in autumn

- the markets selling fresh produce

- the clean, crisp air

She quickly formed friendships in their new neighbourhood. Canadian hospitality, she discovered, was warm in a subtle, gentle way—so different from the exuberant gatherings of her Bahraini and Kuwaiti friends, yet still welcoming.

Julie joined: a local walking group; a volunteer circle at a community centre; a small multicultural women's gathering where she shared recipes and stories of Kuwait.

She was surprised to find how much the other women loved hearing about the Gulf. They asked endless questions about life in Kuwait, Middle Eastern culture, and the extraordinary experiences David and Julie had lived through.

Canada did not replace Kuwait in her heart. But it gave her peace. It gave her space. It gave her a soft, steady life—something she hadn't felt since before the invasion.

As autumn settled over Waterloo and David walked across campus with a folder under his arm, he realised how far he had come:

- from maritime apprentice

- to dredging superintendent

- to hostage

- to builder of a marine division

- and now, to university lecturer

Julie, meanwhile, had created a new circle of friends and routines, finding purpose in community work and sharing her multicultural experiences with Canadians eager to learn. They were thousands of miles from Kuwait, and yet they felt at home.

Yet another chapter of their lives had begun—quiet, steady, hopeful.

Scott's Rise in the Financial World

By **2003**, Scott had firmly established himself in London's financial sector. What began as an ambitious graduate analyst programme had grown steadily into a remarkable career trajectory—one driven by discipline, sharp instinct, and a relentless work ethic.

Working in the sleek glass towers of **Canary Wharf**, Scott quickly became known as someone who could see patterns in markets before others noticed them. His natural talent for valuation, risk assessment, and negotiation led to a rapid series of promotions.

By his early 30s, he was appointed **Head of Acquisition** at his firm—an astonishing achievement for someone so young. He oversaw multimillion-pound deals, advised on key mergers, and led teams with a poise that even his senior colleagues admired.

The hours were long, the pressure unrelenting, but Scott thrived in that environment. He often told David:

"Dad, this isn't stress—this is where I come alive."

David smiled every time. He understood. Ambition, when fuelled by purpose, could be exhilarating.

After several successful years in London, Scott was offered a prestigious role with a major **German investment bank** headquartered in Frankfurt. They wanted him to lead a new strategic acquisitions unit.

It was an opportunity few could refuse global influence, a broader portfolio, and a level of responsibility that only solidified his reputation as an exceptional financial mind.

So, Scott moved to **Frankfurt**, embracing a new culture, a new language, and a highly competitive European market. The German financial scene was more structured, more conservative, yet Scott's dynamic approach fitted surprisingly well.

He once joked to Julie over the phone: "German's love rules, Mum. And I love breaking them in ways that make money."

Marriage to a Successful Trader

While in Frankfurt, Scott met **Elena**, a brilliant trader specialising in secondaries. She was sharp, articulate, fearless in negotiations, and known for her unusually calm temperament during market turbulence.

Their relationship was one of equals—two driven minds pushing each other to be better, stronger, smarter.

They married in a private ceremony attended by close friends and family. David and Julie were immensely proud. Elena fit seamlessly into their lives, and Julie was delighted to have a daughter-in-law she could admire both intellectually and personally.

A Mews House in Chelsea — A Symbol of Success

In 2001, after returning to London for a new position with an international fund manager, Scott and Elena purchased a stunning **mews house in Chelsea**—a quintessential symbol of success in the city:

- cobblestone lane

- pastel-coloured façade

- modern, airy interior

- two floors of carefully designed spaces

- a private terrace perfect for summer evenings

It became their haven during whirlwind careers, a place where friends gathered for dinners, where David and Julie stayed during visits, and where Scott felt he had finally "made it."

He once told David:

"Dad, if you'd told me at 18 that I'd own a place like this... I'd have laughed."

David replied with quiet pride, "You built it piece by piece, son. You earned every brick of it."

Thoughts of Early Retirement Before 50

Despite—or perhaps because of—the high-intensity world he moved in, Scott eventually began thinking beyond finance. The industry was rewarding, but it demanded sacrifices: endless travel, unpredictable markets, stressful negotiations, and the constant pressure to outperform.

By his mid-40s, the conversations changed.

"When I hit 50," Scott confided one evening over dinner in Chelsea, "I want to step back. I've made enough. I want to enjoy life while I'm young enough to really live it."

He spoke of:

- travelling

- investing independently

- teaching finance or mentoring young talent

- spending more time with his parents

- perhaps even buying a home in the countryside

He didn't say it explicitly, but David sensed the deeper truth: Scott didn't want to burn out or lose himself to a career, no matter how lucrative.

Julie listened with tears in her eyes. "He's done so well," she whispered to David later. "He deserves a life. A full life."

Scott's story had become a testament to resilience and ambition—not unlike his father's but carved in a very different world.

And as he looked ahead to the possibility of retiring before turning fifty, it wasn't an escape he envisioned, but rather a transition… …toward a life shaped by choice, freedom, and the rewards he had earned through years of extraordinary dedication.

Chapter 17 – A difficult choice

David and Julie genuinely loved Canada. Waterloo had given them peace, purpose, and kindness at a time when they both needed it most. David found fulfilment in teaching, and Julie had built a warm circle of friends and routines that grounded her. Life there was calm, predictable, and safe.

But there was one thing neither of them could truly make peace with. The winters.

Each year they tried to convince themselves they would adapt, but the cold was relentless. Long months of snow, ice, and grey skies weighed heavily on them— physically and emotionally. David, who had spent much of his working life in warm coastal regions, found the cold increasingly hard on his joints. Julie missed the sun, the light, and the ease of outdoor life they had known for so many years. One evening, as they watched snow fall heavily outside their living-room window, Julie finally said what they were both thinking.

"I don't think this is where we're meant to grow old."

David nodded slowly. "I've been thinking the same thing."

Not long after that conversation, David received a call from an old contact in Kuwait—someone he had worked closely with during the Mushreef years. The voice on the other end was warm, familiar, and direct.

"We could use you again," the man said. "Consultancy only. No long-term operational responsibility. Just your experience." The offer was attractive: a senior **consultancy role**, generous remuneration, flexible terms, and—most importantly—a return to a climate and culture they both knew well. David discussed it at length with Julie.

Kuwait had shaped their lives profoundly. It had given them opportunity, friendships, hardship, and survival. The thought of returning stirred mixed emotions—but also a sense of familiarity and unfinished business.

In the end, the decision felt practical rather than dramatic.

In **February 2002**, they packed their belongings once more. The home they had bought in Canada was **rented out**, carefully managed, left not as a closed chapter but as a door they could one day reopen if needed.

When the aircraft lifted off, Julie looked down at the frozen landscape below.

"I'll miss it," she said softly.

"So will I," David replied. "But I think we're making the right choice."

Dark Clouds on the Horizon

As they settled back into life in Kuwait, the atmosphere was noticeably different from before. There was an undercurrent of tension—quiet, but unmistakable.

International news grew darker by the week.

The United States, under **President George W. Bush,** was increasingly vocal about Iraq. Old grievances resurfaced. The attempted assassination of Bush's father years earlier was never far from the rhetoric, and Saddam Hussein was again being cast as the central villain.

The language was familiar. Weapons. Threats. Ultimatums.

David listened carefully, remembering all too well how quickly words could turn into war. He said to Julie one evening, as the news played quietly in the background: "It feels like history repeating itself."

Julie felt a chill that had nothing to do with climate.

They had returned to Kuwait seeking warmth and familiarity—but once again, the world seemed to be drifting toward conflict. And deep down, both knew that Kuwait, because of its geography and its past, would once again stand dangerously close to the centre of it all.

Reviving a Hopper Dredger

David's first consultancy assignment after returning to Kuwait was both familiar and fitting. The company that engaged him was one he had worked for in his early years in the Gulf—an organisation with solid assets but ageing operational practices. Their concern was clear and urgent.

One of their **trailing suction hopper dredgers**, once reasonably productive, was now underperforming badly. Downtime was excessive, fuel consumption was high, and daily production figures had fallen far below what the vessel should have been capable of achieving.

David was asked a simple question:

"Can you help us to get her working productively again?"

David began the way he always had—by observing rather than judging.

He spent several days onboard the dredger, watching entire dredging cycles from start to finish:

Sailing to the borrow area, positioning over the dredge line, lowering suction arms, loading the hopper, sailing to the disposal site, bottom dumping, returning to position, rainbowing techniques.

He spoke with everyone: the captain, the dredgemasters, the engineers, the deck crew, even the cook. Every man had a piece of the puzzle.

What David found was not incompetence, but inefficiency.

Poor coordination between bridge and engine room, incorrect loading parameters, outdated dredging techniques, incorrect operating speeds, long delays between cycles, preventable maintenance downtime.

Most importantly, the crew were operating on habit rather than data.

Using technology and experience, David returned to shore with notebooks full of observations and figures. Back at his temporary office, he turned to the tools he had mastered years earlier.

He built detailed **spreadsheet models** to analyse:

- cycle times
- loading rates
- fuel burn per cubic metre of freight
- hopper utilisation
- sailing speeds versus output
- maintenance intervals

He overlaid these figures with best-practice data drawn from comparable dredgers he had managed in the past.

Then he created a revised operational model—showing exactly how the dredger could increase production by **30 to 40 percent** without any major capital expenditure.

Implementing Change

David presented his findings to the company's senior management and vessel officers. Rather than criticising, he framed his recommendations as opportunities.

"This dredger doesn't need new equipment," he told them. "She needs a new way of being run."

He proposed: revised dredging cycles, optimised sailing speeds, improved bridge–engine room communication protocols, preventative maintenance scheduling, performance-based crew targets, daily production reporting.

Reluctance gave way to interest. Interest turned into cautious optimism.

When the changes were implemented, results came quickly.

Within weeks: cycle times shortened, daily output increased significantly, fuel consumption per cubic metre dropped, crew morale improved, management confidence returned.

By the end of the second month, the dredger was producing figures close to her original design capacity.

A Reputation Rebuilt

The company's director shook David's hand. "You've given us back a vessel we feared was finished," he said.

For David, the success was deeply satisfying—not just financially, but personally. It reaffirmed that his value lay not only in managing projects, but in **diagnosing problems, mentoring crews, and unlocking hidden performance**.

Word spread quickly. Other companies began asking for his advice. Other dredger operators wanted audits. Other managers wanted "a David-style review."

His consultancy career in Kuwait had begun exactly as it should have: with quiet competence, practical solutions, and measurable results.

Warden

Not long after his return to Kuwait, David was approached discreetly by a senior staff member from the **British Embassy**. The request was unusual but carefully framed. Would he be willing to act as a **warden** for a designated section of the British expatriate community?

The role carried **no salary and no formal status**, but it came with responsibility. In the event of a crisis, David would act as a point of contact—passing on official information, accounting for people in his area, and helping to coordinate assistance if evacuation or shelter became necessary.

The request was not made lightly.

The Embassy was acutely aware of the damage done to its reputation during the **1990 Iraqi invasion**, when many British expatriates felt abandoned, misinformed, or poorly advised. Conflicting messages, delayed responses, and an over-reliance on recorded announcements had left deep resentment within the community—resentment that lingered more than a decade later.

This time, the Embassy wanted **eyes and ears on the ground**. People who were known, trusted, experienced, and capable of remaining calm under pressure.

David fitted that profile perfectly.

He knew Kuwait intimately. He had lived through the invasion. He had been taken hostage. He understood fear, confusion, and the consequences of poor communication better than most.

When the proposal was put to him, David asked only one question: "Will this actually help people?"

The Embassy official replied honestly. "We believe it will. And we need people like you."

David didn't answer immediately. He went home and discussed it with Julie.

She listened carefully, her expression thoughtful—and a little worried.

"You've already been through so much," she said quietly. "I don't want you dragged into something that puts you at risk again."

David nodded. "I know. But I also know what it's like when there's no one telling the truth. No one explaining what's really happening."

Julie took his hand. "If you do this... promise me one thing."

"What's that?"

"That if things start to feel wrong, we leave. No hesitation this time."

He squeezed her hand gently. "I promise." And so, David agreed.

He became a **voluntary warden**, responsible for maintaining contact with British nationals in his sector—keeping lists updated, checking on vulnerable individuals, and acting as a conduit between the Embassy and the community.

It was a quiet role. Mostly phone calls, emails, reassurance, and occasional briefings. But beneath it lay a serious purpose: to ensure that, this time, people would not feel alone or abandoned if the worst happened again.

For David, it wasn't about loyalty to government or flag.

It was about responsibility—to people who, like him once, might one day find themselves in the wrong place at the wrong time, desperately needing clarity, honesty, and a steady voice.

And as the political climate darkened once more, that role would soon prove far more important than anyone initially imagined.

The Open Letter

As tensions continued to rise and the language coming from Washington and London grew increasingly aggressive, David felt a deep and familiar unease. He had seen this path before—heard the same certainty, the same moral absolutes, the same selective intelligence presented as fact. And this time, he could not remain silent.

Drawing on his experience in the region, his knowledge of Kuwait and Iraq, and his own history as a former hostage, David wrote an **open letter addressed to George W. Bush and Tony Blair**. It was calm, reasoned, and respectful—but unmistakably critical.

He questioned the rush toward war. He challenged the certainty with which claims about **weapons of mass destruction** were being presented. He warned of unintended consequences—not only for Iraq, but for the wider Middle East and for ordinary people who would bear the cost of political decisions made far away.

The letter was not inflammatory. It was not ideological. It was written by someone who had lived with the consequences of war.

The **Arab Times** in Kuwait agreed to publish it.

Once it appeared in print, the response was immediate. Some expatriates thanked him quietly. Others warned him he was "rocking the boat." Within official circles, the reaction was far less subtle.

The Liaison Meeting

At the next liaison meeting between the British Embassy and the expatriate wardens, the atmosphere was noticeably strained. David could feel it as soon as he entered the room.

After the formalities were over, the British Ambassador asked David to stay behind. The door closed softly.

The ambassador spoke first, his tone measured but unmistakably disapproving.

"David, your letter has been noted," he said. "I must tell you—it is not helpful to criticise our government at a time like this."

David did not raise his voice. He did not argue emotionally. He simply asked one question.

"Ambassador," he said evenly, "do you genuinely believe the claims being made about Iraq possessing nuclear weapons?"

The room fell silent.

The ambassador hesitated—just briefly—but it was enough.

"That is not the point," he replied. "Our role is to support government policy."

David nodded slowly.

"So, you don't know," he said. "Or you do know, and you're choosing not to say."

The ambassador's expression hardened. "This conversation is inappropriate," he said. "And I must remind you that as a warden, you represent the Embassy."

David met his gaze calmly. "No," he said. "I represent people. British citizens who deserve honesty—not slogans."

From that moment on, the relationship deteriorated rapidly.

David was no longer seen as a cooperative volunteer, but as a **problem**—someone who asked uncomfortable questions and refused to repeat lines he did not believe.

Meetings became formal and cold. Information flowed past him rather than through him. The trust that had once existed evaporated almost overnight.

But David felt no regret. He later said to Julie, quietly: "If asking for the truth makes me inconvenient, then so be it." The letter marked a clear turning point. David had crossed an invisible line—from helpful intermediary to outspoken critic.

And while the Embassy closed ranks, David remained convinced that history would judge the situation differently than the rhetoric of the moment.

He had seen war up close. He had lived with its consequences. And he knew, with absolute certainty, that once it began—no one would truly control where it ended. The storm was coming. And this time, he was determined not to be silent about it.

Early 2003 — The Final Warning

Early in **2003**, the message from the **British Foreign Office** was no longer ambiguous. Official advisories urged all British citizens in Kuwait to **prepare to leave immediately**. The language was stark, stripped of diplomacy and reassurance.

The conclusion had already been reached in London and Washington.

Saddam Hussein had to be removed.

For Julie, the warning struck like a physical blow. The memories of 1990 surged back—fear, helplessness, waiting for news that never came.

"This is happening again," she said one evening, her voice tight with anxiety. "We must leave, David. We *must* leave."

David listened carefully, but his view had not changed.

"There are no nuclear weapons," he said firmly. "Not in Iraq. Not now. I know the region. I know the systems. This is politics, not reality."

Julie shook her head, tears welling in her eyes. "That doesn't matter. What matters is what they *believe*. And what they're willing to do because of it."

For the first time in many years, they stood on opposite sides of a decision—both acting from experience but seeing the danger differently.

With their homes in **Scotland and Canada already sold**, there was no obvious place of refuge. Julie decided to return to Scotland temporarily, staying with friends while she figured out what came next.

Leaving Kuwait this time was painful—not dramatic, but heavy with unspoken fear. At the airport, Julie held David tightly. "Promise me you'll be careful," she said.

"I will," he replied. "And I'll come back as soon as this madness settles."

Neither of them said what they were both thinking: that war, once unleashed, rarely obeys timetables.

Julie travelled to Scotland and, after several unsettled weeks moving between friends' homes, was offered the rental of a **small, single-storey, one-bedroom house in Inverness**. It wasn't grand, very simple in fact, but it was safe, warm, and hers if she wanted it. She accepted without hesitation.

David remained in Kuwait throughout the invasion of Iraq.

As coalition forces gathered and the first strikes began, the atmosphere was tense but strangely controlled. Air-raid sirens sounded intermittently. Military traffic increased. Patriot missile batteries stood ready.

David watched events unfold with a grim sense of inevitability.

He did not believe the justification for war—but he knew how it would be fought.

He stayed indoors when advised, kept his communications discreet, and maintained contact with expatriates still in the country. His experience had taught him caution—but not panic.

When Baghdad fell and Saddam Hussein went into hiding, the initial phase of hostilities was declared over. Kuwait exhaled.

The war had begun elsewhere now. And it was to later show that the Brits and the Americans had done something that Persia, now Iran, could not do in almost two thousand years of rivalry, - dominate arch enemy of Iraq with Shia rule and overwhelming influence. And alarmingly so, giving birth to Daesh and Islamic fundamentalism as neve seen before that would spread throughout the world.

Return and Reflection Only after the bombing subsided and the immediate danger passed did David leave Kuwait and return to Scotland to join Julie.

When he stepped into the small Inverness house, Julie met him at the door and held him for a long time without speaking.

They had survived—again.

David later reflected quietly that history would judge the war differently from the speeches that had justified it. There were no nuclear weapons. No imminent threat. Only consequences that would ripple outward for decades.

Julie, meanwhile, was simply grateful he was home.

For both of them, the events of early 2003 marked the end of an era—a final severing from the Middle East as a place of long-term residence.

They had seen war twice from the front row. Enough was enough.

After a lifetime shaped by movement, risk, and resilience, they finally arrived at the simplest and most enduring truth: peace is found not in where you live, but in who you live it with.

INDEX

Printed in Dunstable, United Kingdom